Spiritual Manifestos

SPIRITUAL MANIFESTOS

Visions for Renewed
Religious Life in America
from Young Spiritual Leaders
of Many Faiths

Edited by Niles Elliot Goldstein
Preface by Martin E. Marty

Walking Together, Finding the Way

SKYLIGHT PATHS Publishing
WOODSTOCK, VERMONT

Spiritual Manifestos:

Visions for Renewed Religious Life in America from Young Spiritual Leaders of Many Faiths

Copyright © 1999 by Niles Elliot Goldstein

Library of Congress Cataloging-in-Publication Data

Spiritual manifestos : visions for renewed religious life in America from young spiritual leaders of many faiths / edited by Niles Goldstein.

p.   cm.

ISBN 1-893361-09-8 (hc)

1. United States—Religion.   2. Spiritual life.   I. Goldstein, Niles Elliot, 1966–

BL2525.S59 1999

200´.973´09049—dc21

                                                                                    99-045025

First Edition

10 9 8 7 6 5 4 3 2 1

Manufactured in the United States of America

Jacket design: Tom Nihan Design
Text design: Graphic Identity, Inc.

Walking Together, Finding the Way

Published by SkyLight Paths Publishing
A Division of LongHill Partners, Inc.
Sunset Farm Offices, Route 4
P.O. Box 237
Woodstock, Vermont 05091
Tel: (802) 457-4000   Fax: (802) 457-4004
www.skylightpaths.com

The Lord said to Abram,

"Go forth from your native land

and from your father's house

to the land that I will show you . . . "

(Genesis 12:1)

CONTENTS

PREFACE

Martin E. Marty
Fairfax M. Cone Distinguished Service Professor Emeritus
The University of Chicago

Let me be eclectic, as the authors of this book tend to be, and introduce it by picking out some words from the title and using them to anticipate the contents.

Beginning at the beginning, and thus appearing to be ordered instead of random and eclectic, let's seize on *Spiritual* and *Manifestos*.

By now the word *Spiritual* has made its mark, bears a cultural stamp, and signals a set of energies that has surprising force at this millennial turn.

It was not always so. While most religious traditions had long spoken of "spiritual" dimensions and maybe even used the word "spirituality," these dimensions and the word had suffered neglect and fallen into disfavor as recently as a third of a century ago. Asked in 1967 to help survey American religion (for the American Academy of Arts and Sciences) by pointing to the "search for a spiritual style in secular America," I found some slight evidence of searches but little favor shown spirituality. The foremost theologian of America at mid-century, Paul Tillich, thought that the word and concept were too worn out, too far dismissed, too remote, ever to reappear.

Soon after, they were back and have become privileged in the discourse of American cultures. "Privileged in the discourse" means that you not only don't have to shuffle and mumble and apologize when using this word and concept, but that you will gain favor by doing so. Listen: "I *hate* organized religion. I am *not* a member of the institutional church. I do not even *like* religion, and I am *not* religious. But I am *very* spiritual." You hear it every day, on television, in campus discussions, among friends, and maybe when listening to yourself.

One of the writers in this book is a bit suspicious of the use of "spirituality" as a counterpoint to "religion." Maybe the spiritual search is just "religion" dolled up and dressed up for a new time. Someone has defined: Spirituality is what is left after you take religion and then take out of it all the things you don't like. It is true that it is encyclopedists of religion who are likely to include in their alphabet of subjects "Spirituality." They see it as a species of the genus "Religion."

Perhaps the words "*religious* manifestos" would kill the book and chase away its potential market. Only in the subtitle is the "R-word" to be sneaked in, as in *Renewed Religious Life.* The authors are sufficiently people of their time—I almost said "children" of their time—to be aware of the negative coloring "religion" or "religious" tends to have on first hearing. They do not fight much over words. They do know that they must somehow capture the attention of people who have privileged a certain discourse or who have walked into a time and place in which that discourse has already been privileged.

The point here is to ask: What are they doing differently about "spirituality"? I'd answer it by reference to a distinction I have found myself making as I observe the searchers. They converge on and give unity to the book by probing what I call "moored" as opposed to "unmoored" spirituality.

"Unmoored" spirituality is entirely free-floating, directionless, enterprising, individualized. You make it up as you go along. You are purely eclectic. You are on the high seas of life—who isn't?—

and there are storms and waves and mists. Now and then the clouds break and you find a polestar, or the glimpse of an island. Then you are tossed and turned. Naming yourself captain of your fate, you boldly take this measure from one map and that from another chart. It is all very daring, quite exciting, and sufficiently rewarding. In any case, the effort beats sinking or being stilled in the waters. The one thing you do not know or have or wish for is a harbor, a mooring.

"Moored" spirituality does not mean being in dry dock or tied to the pier or safely anchored. In its case, you are also on the high seas, amid storms or afraid of being becalmed. But you know there is a destination and a source for further exploration. You have inherited a compass to help you find the mooring again.

Moorings, in such a picture and as portrayed in this book, include communities, traditions, texts, inherited experiences. There is no way these authors could agree on which mooring everyone should cherish, but they demonstrate that they see advantages in spiritual moorings and tell why. They may well represent the advance guard or, to get back to the aquatic metaphor, they may be sailing the flagships, for a generation that sees the limits of the unmoored way.

Second, *Manifestos*. Manifestos are public declarations of principles, policies, and intentions, especially in the political realm. Do these chapters qualify? They are public. No one writes a book and tries to keep knowledge of its existence private. These authors put themselves on the line and declare themselves.

They set forth certain principles, choosing autobiographical modes of outlining them: This is what happened to me or people with whom I associate. Maybe something in this happening can help you organize your life. Policies: When you find a mooring, you will find that the waters around it need dredging, the pillars are rotting and need attention, the boathouse is in shambles. Renew them. Intentions: We intend to be of service to you, the reader, in your search.

This is not a conventional manifesto, since it is not the sort of thing you tack on a bulletin board or a door. There is nothing here of the cocksureness one associates with manifestos. Still, the intention to get attention and the hope that the attentive will find their lives changed mark all the essays.

Next, in the postmodern spirit that these authors share, I'll eclectically focus on the word *Young* in the title. A few minutes ago, it seems, it was 1967 and I belonged to a generation of the then-young who were picking our way among the moorings and sighting the unmoored. Now, a few minutes later, we are retired, and bring the perspective of seven or more decades of life lived to all our observations. One side of me wants to shout to the authors: "Stay at it, and use the time well. Careers, vocations, opportunities, and lives hurtle by." Another side of me prompts encouragement: "At last, a new generation is beginning to emerge. We hope you are typical."

Spiritual sagacity does not belong only to seniors like Mother Teresa and Dorothy Day, Martin Buber and Abraham Joshua Heschel, the veteran Desmond Tutu and the aging Dalai Lama. Let's hear from a generation that is marked by new experiences.

José Ortega y Gasset, his student Julián Marías, Karl Mannheim, and other mentors of our century have taught us to pay attention to generations. They represent cohorts of people who have had common shaping experiences. The World War I generations developed neo-orthodoxies, neo-scholasticisms, or existentialist responses to the horrors of war, the devastations of postwar life and, in America especially, economic depression. Their successors, the post-World War II generations, refined these responses, adapted them, worked for renewal, in the midst of prosperity and the experiences of mid-century life. About the generation of "the sixties," enough said.

No single traumatic experience unites the generation the present authors represent or serve or would serve. Communist empires fell, leaving spiritual deserts. The market won, and material prosperity has left spiritual vacuums. The motives for the spiritual search of the time are mixed, complex, not easily discerned. These authors are giving a voice to some of the yearnings and pointing to some of the ways to define the spiritual search today. This book makes a contribution to the work of all who are trying to discern what is going on in mind and soul and spirit in emerging cultures.

Two words from the title remain and bid for comment: *Many Faiths*. This is a book of moorings, not mooring. It can easily be misread. Because the writers are Jewish and Catholic and Protestant and Buddhist and Unitarian Universalist they represent problems, not solutions, to those who think that one can easily find a mooring and stay in that safe harbor. ("Why not have a manifesto which helps the reader pick a way through all the choices to the right one?")

To change the image, the book could appear to be a sequence of booths set up at a spiritual fair. Come, the chapters bid, and take a look at what we, for all our faults, have to advertise. The searcher can soon grow suspicious: "Is this all advertising?" Or weary: "Why so many stops along the way?" Yet such questions born of slight misreadings miss the point of the book.

One book, said Eugen Rosenstock-Huessy, is about one thing; at least the good ones are. This book is not an apology for the existence of God; two authors are not even in God-traditions. It is not a book in which one will find the Truth, the Absolute, and negation of all falsehoods and relativities. It is one in which the authors demonstrate the values of spiritual moorings and their contributions to the varied adventures that explorers on diverse vessels and courses undertake in efforts not to be shipwrecked and, at the same time, in efforts to get somewhere.

If these authors are collectively of help they merit the term in the title; they are *Leaders*. I hope they are given a wide hearing.

INTRODUCTION

When Martin Luther wanted to get the attention of his peers and what he viewed as a sick Church, he nailed a set of ninety-five theses to a door—and wound up changing the nature of religion in the western world for centuries. Today, most people would have walked past his manifesto or dismissed him as a nut. Too busy to stop and read, too "modern" to take religious doctrine very seriously, most of us see matters of God and faith as irrelevant to our everyday lives.

We have a hard time believing that saying formal prayers and performing ancient rites will somehow better our lives. We question the idea that religious creed or canon law will ennoble us as human beings. For the vast majority of Americans, especially younger Americans, the fiery passion that animated Luther and others like him—a passion that in many cases led to certain death—seems incomprehensible. What to our forebears was a sacred treasure has become to us just another remnant of a past we discard like junk mail.

Yet while most of us have turned our backs on the religions of our parents and grandparents, the spiritual impulse continues to express itself in new forms. As many mainline churches and synagogues slouch into the next millennium, both the left-leaning New Age spiritualities as well as the right-leaning fundamentalist movements are experiencing a period of tremendous growth and explosive zeal. They speak to people in ways that traditional religious institutions rarely do. At the brink of the twenty-first century, the lines between sacred and secular have become blurred.

Most of the current books on spirituality fall into one of two camps: those written by men and women (like Thomas Moore and

Karen Armstrong) who have worked in but left the active clergy, and those written by outsiders (like the poet Kathleen Norris and the physician Andrew Weil) who essentially observe and analyze matters of the spirit. Very few books of this genre are written by those on the *inside;* those who have, despite society's frequent indifference to its houses of worship and their own personal struggles, retained their faith in and devotion to the traditions and rites of organized religion.

Through the voices of some of America's best and brightest young clergy and religious teachers, *Spiritual Manifestos* confronts the challenges facing mainstream religions. Why are they in trouble? Are they spiritual enough for the present generation? Are they *too* spiritual? Have any attempts to compete with New Age and charismatic groups begun to "dumb down" their own institutions? In what ways have religious communities changed, and how far can they go in creating new ceremonies and rituals to keep in step with the times? How can formal religion reach the hearts of a largely secular public? What new vision can revitalize some of our most sacred traditions and save them from social extinction? As young spiritual leaders, we're well aware of these issues and problems. And we've dedicated our lives to trying to deal with them.

This collection of visions is *our* manifesto, our attempt to reach not the converted, but all those among us who break into cold sweats whenever they walk through the front doors of our churches, synagogues, and zendo. We understand their hesitation. These people are our peers, our friends, sometimes even our family members. In a postmodern world, a world in which so many of the institutions we once viewed as impervious have crumbled before our eyes, expositions on theology, doctrine, or creed simply don't speak to people. What moves them, even those who aren't "religious," are our stories, our struggles, our visions of a new spirituality that crosses denominational lines and that offers meaning and purpose in a world that seems so fractured and indifferent. Unable—and unwilling—to hide behind dogma anymore, all we can do is share our lives and our views, and open our hearts to those who will listen.

Today's religious teachers look as different from their predecessors as does America from its prior generations. We're not all white. We're not all men. We're different not only in some of the things we have to say, but in who we *are*. From wide-ranging and often starkly different vantage points, these visions describe our individual journeys and display our collective portraits for the transformation of religion and sacred practice. We've each heard the Call, and our missions are before us, even if that means reshaping or reinterpreting our traditions in ways that our forebears couldn't.

Though we speak from within the context of many and varied traditions, all of us share a vision of a new model for religious life in America—one that is passionate and intelligent, elevating and fulfilling, spiritual and contemporary. Just as each of us defies the stereotypical image of a religious leader and teacher, so must our religious institutions defy the preconceptions that most of us have about them. Our goal is to show both the believer and the skeptic that there can be a place for all of us in our houses of worship— regardless of our struggles with faith—if only we'd give them a chance, and that we are infusing our synagogues, churches, and zendo with new creativity and transforming them from the dull and uninspiring institutions that they too often are into welcoming sanctuaries for the spirit where our deepest longings and common needs might be met.

In selecting the contributors for *Spiritual Manifestos*, I sought diversity and excellence. Each is a talented young religious leader and teacher, and all are trying to implement their visions for new spiritual life in America. Most of the contributors are under the age of thirty-five. Three are Jewish, five are Protestant, two are Roman Catholic, and one is a Buddhist. The six men and five women in the book come from a mix of racial and demographic backgrounds. One is African-American. Another is Japanese-American. One vision is written by a married clergy couple that works in the same parish.

We live in cities from Boston to Anchorage. Most of us are members of the congregational clergy, but some of us have chosen to express our spiritual commitments in other ways. We're just like you: We struggle with faith. We're looking for answers to life's questions. But we've chosen to devote our lives to changing, improving, and expanding spiritual life in America. It is my hope that with *Spiritual Manifestos* all generations of spiritual seekers—postmodern, multicultural, freethinking—will begin to look at organized religion in new ways and together usher in a new era of religious awakening and revitalization.

—Niles Elliot Goldstein
Brooklyn, New York

SPIRITUAL DINING AT THE AMERICAN CAFÉ

Father Brett C. Hoover

In all honesty, I am one of those silly people who felt the call to be a priest almost

from the womb. (Okay, really maybe the fourth grade.) Early on in

elementary school, I had a dream one night that Jesus' face appeared on

the large altar of a

Methodist church some-

where in the Northeast.

In the dream I was

watching it on TV. What

possible significance or

connection this had to the priesthood, I don't know, but to a fourth grader

it was proof positive of a vocation to the priesthood. By the way, it was

many years before I realized that Methodist churches don't have giant

altars!

Through the years, my sense of call waxed and waned, depending on

friends' opinions, current anxieties, other hobbies and interests, and, of

course, hormones. Through it all, the religious heritage and foundation

of my family remained firmly planted within me, though it changed and developed. Eventually I found myself at St. Mark's University Parish in Santa Barbara, California, under the guidance of several Paulist priests. The Paulists are an order of Catholic priests founded in the United States in the mid-nineteenth century with a very optimistic sense of the ability of Roman Catholicism and American culture to get along. Their spirit has remained progressive and energetic, and their practical, down-to-earth spirituality captivated me. After two years of the post-college working grind, I joined the Paulists and studied theology for four years at the Washington Theological Union in Washington, D.C. Then I had a year-long internship at the Catholic campus ministry center for the University of California at Berkeley, and shortly after that I finished my first book, Losing Your Religion, Finding Your Faith: Spirituality for Young Adults.

After ordination in 1997, I found myself in New York City at St. Paul the Apostle Church, where I work with a Spanish-speaking community from all over the Americas. The cultural misunderstandings constantly challenge us to let go of our individual and cultural expectations to see what is really possible together. I also go about the usual work of parish ministry—baptizing and preaching, counseling and teaching, visiting the sick and burying the dead. I am repeatedly amazed and humbled by the magic that happens when people of faith gather together!

All religion and spirituality ought to be zesty, passionate, rich, and deep. I have been privileged to experience all this in Roman Catholicism. This lively faith experience has challenged my assumptions, touched my heart, and made me grow up. Perhaps most important, my faith has brought me together with other people who are passionately seeking God. To sum it up, my experience is that religion done well makes people's worlds bigger, not smaller. That's what I see working in the programs and situations that find a home in this chapter. That is my wish for everyone with some kind of hunger of the spirit.

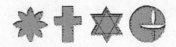

America is hungry.

Lest this sound like the beginning of a breakfast cereal commercial ("America is hungry for . . . Cocoa Puffs"), let me clarify: Some of us are actually physically hungry, as in malnourished. But there is a different sort of hunger, a metaphorical malnourishment that is not satisfied by fortified breakfast cereals. Americans crave meaning, something deep and intangible that has been misplaced along our merry secular way.

Symptoms of this hunger? Books like *Conversations with God* and *The Celestine Prophecy* frequently appear on the *New York Times*' best-seller list. Televangelists continue to draw an audience, despite the prominent downfall of so many a decade ago. Words and phrases like karma, Zen, "my next life," inner peace, and nirvana have become common. Huge, evangelical Christian "megachurches" draw in countless disconnected suburbanites. Christian symbols are fashion statements for teenagers. Yoga and meditation classes are now found beyond just New York and California. And even though the traditional churches are not so full as they once were, polls show Americans overwhelmingly believe in God.

The word these days is not religion but spirituality. People are hungry for it, though the secularization of our society has left many of us with little background on the subject. And so we read, talk, study, flip on the TV, submit ourselves to teachers and gurus and pilgrimages, even attend seemingly incomprehensible services to get it. But what is this spirituality and how is it different (if, indeed, it is different) from the religion of our grandparents and great-grandparents? Is spirituality just religion dressed up for the turn of the millennium? Is it a basic belief in more than just what we see? Is it a reason to get up in the morning? Is it living in harmony with all that is?

A survey of the world's most ancient religious traditions will turn up at least several of these answers—and more—in reference to spirituality. The wonderful and confusing thing about the realm of faith and spirituality is that many answers and questions can be simultaneously (and sometimes paradoxically) held together in a kind of patchwork quilt of meaning.

At nineteen, I began my own Southern California kind of spiritual quest. A baptized and confirmed Catholic, I nevertheless embarked on a course that included study and discussion of not only my own faith but of much Eastern religion that I had first learned about through the New Age movement in the early 1980s. I meditated and went to Mass, speculated on possible past lives and became an active member of my local Catholic parish. I discussed modern philosophy (of which I knew zero) and shamanism with my priest, a cultural anthropologist by training. Never did I see a contradiction in these things. And thank God I didn't. I was experimenting in spirituality, trying various "spiritual foods," in search, though I did not know it yet, of a deeper and more nuanced view of God, one that could give me perspective and strength in a very complicated world. Eventually I found I had to concentrate my energies in one direction, lest I forever remain adolescently scattered. So I chose my own religious tradition. But the surveying I had done extended the boundaries of my spiritual tastes and did me good.

I was, as are many Americans, hungry for spirituality. Our life has become more materially comfortable, but also more crass, compartmentalized, and sanitized. One can avoid dealing with the messy human realities (birth, family, community, death, sickness) that naturally lead to spiritual thoughts. Religion and talk about God have not disappeared; they just too often (and I blame both religion and culture for this) seem to have nothing to do with our everyday life. But even so, the need for spirituality does not disappear. When everything is bought and paid for (or appropriately mortgaged), what else do we want from life? What lies below the practical, commercial surface? Where do I go when the deeper questions of meaning and the longing for connection won't go away?

From Junk Food to Elegant Spiritual Dining

O ne of the spiritual challenges of our cultural moment is that too many people, perhaps out of a suspicion of institutions, are limiting their spiritual search to the great commercial vending machines of spiritual junk food. You loved *The Celestine Prophecy*? You are entertained by your local megachurch's multimedia sermons? Great, no problem. Both, however, are watered-down versions of ancient traditions, a reduction of enormously rich and complicated spiritual traditions to a few nifty soundbites. Do any of these really teach us anything about life that will still be with us twenty years from now? Do they help us survive a father's death or keep us from having a mental breakdown when tragedy strikes? In other words, there is absolutely nothing wrong with these types of spirituality except that they are superficial and give you nice, sentimental phrases to soothe you and make you feel good now. But do they challenge you in any way? Do they really make you a more loving person?

The strongest and deepest spiritualities the world can offer still come from the world's great religions. In Tony Kushner's epic drama about AIDS, *Angels in America,* a conversation between a secular Jew and his Mormon boyfriend ends up with the Jewish character claiming that Mormonism is not a real religion because "anything that's not at least 2,000 years old is a cult, and I know some people who would call that generous!" Whether or not this is true (I know too little of Mormonism to judge), it gets at why the Great Religions have the richest fare—experience. Like Jacob in Genesis, ancient religious traditions have been around long enough to have really wrestled with God (and with spirituality). Any religion whose only answer about why there is evil in the world is that white devils came along or that Satan controls the United Nations needs to get a life! This does not cut the spiritual mustard! Human beings need enough ingredients (both questions and answers) surrounding the quest for the answer to evil (traditionally called theodicy) to serve themselves an uncomfortable yet elegant feast of meaning. "Why spend your money for what is not bread, your wages for what fails to satisfy?" reasonably asked the Hebrew prophet Isaiah 2,500 years ago. Junk-food religion is amusing once in a while, but it is not nourishing.

Of course, there's a whole lot of junk food even within the great religious traditions as well. Ask a "recovering" Catholic about obsessive sexual guilt or a Muslim professional woman about "fundamentalist" ideas of how women gain holiness. So how do you get to the good stuff? The first challenge is finding a good church, synagogue, or mosque. The first stop on that road is, of course, worship. Traditionally, we Catholics were on notice to go to the closest parish, the one within whose geographical boundaries we lived. Maybe this worked in an earlier, more stable era. It's time for Catholics to be okay with "church shopping." By using this metaphor, I am not advocating attending a house of worship where you "feel comfortable" at worship. Doing this means we are surrendering once again to a commercial view of religion. Instead, to get the most out of the experience, we need to find worship that is lively, that makes us think, that engages our hearts and bodies as well as our minds. So, first of all, get away from the zombie churches of the dead where organs play at dirgelike speeds. Get away from the feel-good, entertaining churches. Find a place with life, faith, and depth. Find a place with authentic community. In my experience, there's always a place to go. It needn't be perfect, as long as there's some life in it.

Hungry for Community

We are hungry, but the hunger in our deepest heart is not just for some sense of spirituality. Along with spirituality always comes community. As human beings, we were made for one another, for loving each other in a hundred different ways. Yet the U.S. at the turn of the millennium could conceivably be the loneliest place on earth. Think about it: Young adults and the elderly living alone in the city; single parents; neighbors you hardly know; people always moving away from their extended families. What has happened to community? How did we lose track of one another? It's probably the dark side of our obsession with individual freedom. Ever since the dawn of the Republic, our nation has embodied the drive for an individual's rights and independence. This has led to a nation with unprecedented mobility and freedom of expression as well as the creativity and enterprise that go with them. But everything has a cost, and the cost of this individualism has been the loss of a sense of community. We have great individual striving, but too often there is great longing and emptiness inside.

Believe it or not, I think faith communities provide one of the most reliable antidotes to our fractured sense of belonging. Everything is a "community" in our politically correct discourse, but how many "communities" have much depth? Too often we're talking about superficial conversation, shared lifestyle expectations, material focus, and not much depth. Where can people go to make a deeper connection? Why not go to a house of worship? Here in New York, I swear it's one of the few alternatives to bars that I hear about when I ask engaged couples where they met. For those who find a social circle in a faith community, there is friendship, shared questions and faith, shared values and vision. Churches can be a kind of "alternative family" for people. I have seen more than one burned, frightened, young adult come alive again once immersed in the friendships formed at church. But again, not just any church will do. Look for life! Find a place with diversity and energy and true worship.

Finding the Good Food

Here at my parish in Manhattan, St. Paul the Apostle, people come from as far as Brooklyn and Queens, even from the New Jersey suburbs, to attend worship services and be a part of the community of faith. That sounds like I'm bragging, but it's just an example of what can happen when there is life in a place. We are far from perfect (we definitely need to focus more on justice issues), but we do have vibrant music, some ethnic and socio-economic diversity, a great deal of lay participation, and preaching that tries to make the connection between Catholic tradition and our everyday life. The worship life of our parish is our number one priority: It's where we see the greatest number of people. But worship is also a doorway into the other activities offered by the parish, such as adult religious education, discussions on spirituality, book discussion groups, prayer, and retreat experiences. These are the beginnings of a house of worship's response to people's hunger for spirituality and community. Through these, people meet one another, talk, and make connections that last.

Something for Seekers and Returners

Having said that, we ought to face reality. Church activities are usually for people who already know where to look for spirituality and community; they are a gourmet supermarket for those who can afford it. Yet all is not lost. There are, in the Catholic tradition, programs and processes that address the needs of those not so terribly involved. Since the Second Vatican Council in the 1960s, the Catholic Church has established a process of gradual inclusion for seekers who are checking out the Church. It's called the Rite of Christian Initiation for Adults (in church jargon, RCIA) and can be found at many (though not all) Catholic churches in the U.S. Done well, it truly represents a non-threatening exploration of how Catholic tradition can speak to the deepest longings of the human heart. More recently, a number of "re-entry" programs have blossomed for those who grew up more or less Catholic but have been away from regular practice for a long time. Our parish has Landings, an excellent ten-week group process where folks alienated from the faith they were raised in join veteran Catholics (often former "returnees") in talking about the spiritual struggles of their lives and finding out if—and what—Catholic tradition can say to those struggles. It's meant to be a low-pressure, welcoming atmosphere.

The limitation of Landings and other re-entry programs is that they are aimed at people who are "alienated from the Church." This turns out to be almost exclusively middle-class baby boomers who, of course, are only a small part of the human race, even the Catholic human race. As for other humans, I'd like to focus on a couple of groups here.

In Chicago, for example, Father John Cusick of the Catholic archdiocese has turned downtown parishes into "young adult centers" that attract so-called "Generation Xers" in their twenties and early thirties. His claim is that traditional parish logistics are centered on stability and the status quo. To work with younger people, you have to be willing to operate around their incredible mobility. At Old St. Patrick's in Chicago, they do just that, and the success is tangible. Their "Theology on Tap" series attracts Gen-Xers in great numbers, not only for beer and fraternization, but for discussion on topics of importance and spiritual relevance. The program is being copied around the country.

Another spiritual "entry point" for younger seekers is university campus ministry. College students are probably spiritually hungrier than most, since most of them are intellectually, emotionally, and morally experimenting. Also, away from home, they are looking for deeper connections and community. In the midst of the swirling chaos of university life, a campus ministry center can provide a safe space and resources for getting one's spiritual act together in a new and more independent way. At the University of California at Berkeley, the Catholic campus ministry center at Newman Hall is a thriving, active place where students come together for social, service, and spiritual activities. The activities are chosen and led by a peer leadership group with the support and guidance of the priests and professional staff (including women, which is very important in a religion where women are not clergy). Each of the activities, from retreats to the weekly spaghetti dinner, is run by a team of student volunteers. Through these, students bond with one another, struggle with their faith, and learn collaborative leadership skills that they can use in the church and in the world of tomorrow.

Catholic Gays and Lesbians?

A perhaps surprising cutting-edge Catholic re-entry ministry is directed at gays and lesbians. Everyone knows that the Catholic Church traditionally teaches against homosexual sex. Few know, however, of the various local and national attempts to accept gay and lesbian seekers in Catholic communities. Many gay men and lesbians are fed up with the superficial atmosphere of some urban gay neighborhoods and want a deeper spirituality and a more diverse community experience. Unfortunately, too often they have found that they are not welcome in faith communities. Miracle of miracles, however, in urban (and some suburban) areas, a few Catholic parishes have established ministries of welcome for gay men and lesbians. The best of these focus on living a life of spirituality and community. They don't overemphasize sexual issues. They aim to integrate folks into the life of the parish. This inevitably causes some controversy. Certain diehards still see any outreach to gay people as wrong, but thankfully, most Catholics are now happy (and sometimes even a bit curious) to be attending church and ministering beside gay folks.

The eventual result of all these local efforts (and a larger outreach program from the Catholic Diocese of Los Angeles) is a scattering of Catholic dioceses and parishes with gay and lesbian outreach programs. On a national level, the U.S. Catholic bishops offered a positively toned pastoral letter entitled, "Always Our Children" (1998). Defying stereotypes about gays as exiles from their families, the bishops called upon parents and families to accept and cherish their gay and lesbian children, not to try to change them but to love them unconditionally as Jesus taught.

Dining with the Different

Back to food. There is a particular meal that many Americans would rather not attend but that we desperately need—the communal supper of cultural and racial reconciliation. Our national rhetoric and some national and state laws reflect a quest for equality and unity among a diversity of people. But our national behavior is a little behind our rhetoric and our statutes: "Sorry, I would love to cross cultural and racial lines to dine with those who are different from me, but I just have other plans tonight." It's challenging and frustrating to approach our differences as a nation, and most people want to be with their own kind; at times, they *need* to be with their own kind so they can build up political will and strength among their own folks.

But still, hungry or not, we need to have this meal of reconciliation. The 1980s and 1990s saw the U.S. become more culturally diverse than ever before in its history. I knew this was true when a priest told me he runs a Catholic mass in Spanish in rural Minnesota! In many cities across the country, there is an increasing amount of ethnic infighting, white flight, and power politics in Catholic parishes. We need to have this meal of reconciliation because we have no choice. We have to begin to deal with one another. On a deeper level, I also wonder about the spiritual cost of our divisions and inexperience with one another. Human beings grow when confronted with that which is different. And, over and above that, spirituality reminds us that we are all ultimately of the same ilk. We are one. In Judeo-Christian language, we are all made in the image and likeness of God (Genesis 1:26). I wonder what diseases of the spirit result from our inability to accept and honor differences and if they will ultimately stunt the spiritual growth of our nation.

Naturally, great religious traditions speak of the underlying unity and common origin of all human beings. They urge us on to peace with one another and to peace within. Surely the best spiritualities they offer—Buddhist universal compassion, Christian love for the neighbor, Jewish concern for the oppressed, Muslim single-minded orientation to an all-loving Creator—can help bring Americans together in the new century. Again, I have to speak from my own tradition of Roman Catholicism. We are perhaps the largest multi-cultural entity in our country. This guarantees no great harmony, and in fact in too many Catholic churches there is resentment and fear among the ethnic groups living there. But, on the other hand, they *do* live there. In church, the opportunity exists to interact, whereas in the broader culture it is so easy to avoid the encounter entirely.

On the positive side, under the Catholic umbrella are countless volunteer programs where young people can work with people of different races and cultures than their own (both here and abroad). Some parishes are beginning to move beyond mere toleration to actually celebrate at mass the languages, music, and customs brought by different cultures to North America. Some parishes even use music and customs from cultures not represented in their community as a way to suggest solidarity with an even greater array of cultures. An interesting strategy comes from the Catholic Diocese of Oakland, California. Once a year, people from throughout the diocese gather for a large mass in which every major culture represented in the area—African-Americans, Koreans, Filipinos, various Latino cultures, and many others—manifests its heritage. It's an impressive experience of diversity for those Catholics who are accustomed to a church experience that is totally assimilated to the mainstream culture, and the richness and variety are mesmerizing.

Supplying Food for the Culture

All of this is great, but still most of it is only available to those who take the trouble to walk through church doors. As the twenty-first century dawns, is there any way faith communities can bring some depth—some spirituality and community perhaps—to the larger (and often superficial) mainstream culture? Can churches, synagogues, zendos, and mosques export their good food? This is a fuzzy area for a young priest to speak of. Some talk about Catholic influence on the media. Too often that amounts to the hysteria of the Catholic League over movies and plays that would get little attention if not for the League's protests. I prefer positive influence. The one initiative I can speak proudly of came from a Catholic priest who is a fellow Paulist. He helped organize (with other religious professionals) the Humanitas prize, which is given to tele-vision writers who come up with stories that embody values usually associated with religion and that explore deeper human issues. Believe it or not, these prizes often go to writers on gritty shows like "NYPD Blue" for their honest handling of human moral dilemmas.

How else can religion affect the larger culture? Drs. Joe and Eileen Connolly, who are organizational and clinical psychologists and friends of mine, offer workshops throughout the world on effective group communication, collaboration, and leadership skills. Such workshops are a dime a dozen these days, but the Connollys' specific goal is to promote moral and spiritually grounded leadership in our society.

Wisdom from the Hungry

Many of us are allergic to organized religion these days, but maybe there's a point of view missing from our American culture that can shed light on why we need religion. In fact, seeing life through another person's eyes opens our own. While studying Spanish in Latin America, I heard more than one preacher or parent of children or teacher or bar companion say that the differ-ence between our two worlds, north and south, is this: The hunger of their people is palpable and physical. But the greatest challenge of the *norteamericanos* is "spiritual poverty." What they mean has to do partially with the fractured and individualist nature of the U.S., which both terrifies and fascinates Latin Americans. But they also know that we are starving for community, and their hospitality is a kind of compassionate pledge they make.

But beyond just the need for company, they read our secular-ism as a kind of spiritual lacuna: "The poor Americans," they say. "They don't even know how to talk about God!" And from their relatives and friends who live here, Latin Americans hear about the incredible material temptations, the cruelty of the economic gap between rich and poor, the lunacy of the rat race, the superficiality and complacency of people who have no religion to guide them. They hear these things and they ask you if they're true. I never know quite how to answer. Perhaps these stories are more true than we would like to admit. There is much good here, too, and we should not forget about that. But like my poorer brothers and sisters south of the border, I think that religion and spirituality do have much to offer hungry Americans. Jesus said, "The poor you will always have with you" (Mark 14:7). Maybe after all these years, it's time we finally started listening to them.

For More Information

Church of St. Paul the Apostle
Columbus Ave. at 60th St.
   in Manhattan
Church office:
415 W. 59th Street
New York, NY 10019
Tel: (212) 265-3495
Website:
   www.stpaultheapostle.org
Sunday masses — Sat. 5:15 P.M.,
Sun. 8 A.M., 10 A.M.,
12:15 P.M. (Spanish), 5:15 P.M.

Landings: Welcoming Returning
   Catholics
Father Jac Campbell, CSP,
   director
5 Park Street
Boston, MA 02108
Tel: (617) 720-5986 or
   (617) 452-7566
E-mail: Campbell@paulist.org
Website:
   www.paulist.org/landings

Office of Young Adult Ministry,
   Archdiocese of Chicago
Father John Cusick, director
122 S. Desplaines
Chicago, IL 60661-3519
Tel: (312) 466-9473

Newman Hall/Holy Spirit
parish — campus ministry
for the University of
California at Berkeley
Father Gilbert Martinez, CSP,
director of campus ministry
2700 Dwight Way
Berkeley, CA 94704
Tel: (510) 848-7813

Ministry with the Lesbian and
Gay Catholics, Archdiocese
of Los Angeles
Father Peter Luizzi, O. Carm.,
director
3424 Wilshire Boulevard
Los Angeles, CA 90010-2241
Tel: (213) 637-7337
E-mail:
frpjluizzi@la-archdiocese. org
Website:
www.mlgc.la-archdiocese.org

Ethnic Pastoral Centers,
Archdiocese of Oakland, CA
2900 Lakeshore Avenue
Oakland, CA 94610
Tel: (510) 893-4711
Fax: (510) 893-0945

Humanitas Prize
Father Ellwood Kieser, CSP,
president;
Mary Williams, executive
director
17575 Pacific Coast Highway
P.O. Box 861
Pacific Palisades, CA 90272
Tel: (310) 454-8769
Fax: (310) 459-6549

Communication Center #1
Drs. Joseph and Eileen Connolly,
directors
214 South Meramec Avenue
St. Louis, MO 63105
Tel: (314) 863-7267
Fax: (314) 863-7263
E-mail: ComCtr1@aol.com

MAKING IT YOURS:
JUDAISM AT THE CROSSROADS

Rabbi Sara Paasche-Orlow

I grew up integrating the Jewish American culture of my mother with the immigrant experience of my father. My father's parents, non-Jews who were in the German resistance, left Germany in 1935 and my father was raised

in Japan. My great-grandfather, Kurt von Hammerstein, was the top commander of the German Army. He abhorred the policies of Hitler and was relieved of his command when Hitler came to power. His later attempt to arrest Hitler at the Polish front was frustrated. He died in 1943. Two of his sons, my great uncles, took part in the July 1944 assassination plot against Hitler. Their mother—my great-grandmother—had been driven out of Germany by the Gestapo in 1935 for aiding the escape of Communists and Jews.

A few decades earlier, my other great-grandfather, an outspoken pacifist, had been a popular leader of the younger generation who were against German imperialism. He was tried for treason and executed in 1921.

From my mother, I inherit a completely secular Jewish identity despite the fact that my great-grandfather was a rabbi who studied at the same seminary where ninety years later I studied. The German language often serves as a bridge between my two diverse histories, letting me speak to German Jews who survived the Holocaust and with a new generation of Christian Germans.

My personal history has taught me to question and challenge established institutions. As a Conservative movement rabbinical student, I worked at a gay and lesbian synagogue, Congregation Beth Simchat Torah, challenging Conservative Judaism to be more tolerant and inclusive of gay and lesbian Jews. After ordination I served for a year as a fellow at CLAL, the Jewish Center for Learning and Leadership, where rabbis from all Jewish denominations work together to create new teachings to promote common ground for differing segments of the Jewish world. The following year I co-founded the Bavli Yerushalmi Project, an effort to create dialogue between diverse American and Israeli Jews with text study as its center. I am currently working at the Jewish Life Network on the idea of promoting service and volunteerism as a gateway for Jewish identity building.

My husband, Dr. Michael Paasche-Orlow, and I share an interest in Jewish medical ethics as they apply to the healthcare system and patient care with a focus on the urban poor. We have two children, Raziel and Lev.

For Judaism to grow, it has to be able to encompass postmodern spiritual seekers. To do this, Judaism must address feminism and ritual meaningfulness, environmentalism and social activism. This calls for a departure from the male-centered, urban Judaism that has focused on the survival of the Jews. Until women's experience is fully in the center alongside that of men, until we have reclaimed a connection to the natural world, until we commit ourselves to repairing our human world, Judaism will limp along into the future, if indeed it has one.

There Are Many Matriarchs of Our Faith

There is a little known character in the Hebrew Bible named Serach. She first appears in the book of Genesis in a genealogical list as a daughter of Asher. This reference is repeated in Numbers and then again in Proverbs. In these lists of almost all men, suddenly a daughter appears. The Ramban, a thirteenth-century rabbi, explains that Serach's mother married Asher when she was already a widow with a daughter, thus the daughter coming from this first marriage was an heir since there were no sons. A woman who stands to inherit is one who has made it into the ranks of the community.

A series of rabbinic stories add to the uniqueness of Serach.

She is said to have played the harp and sang to Jacob to gently tell
the old man that his son Joseph was still alive. She reappears later to
help Moses relocate the coffin of Joseph when the Jews are leaving
Egypt. Like the prophet Elijah, she is said to never have died; rather,
she entered paradise alive.

We now have an opportunity to invite her into our ritual lives.
As an eternal figure, she can offer comfort at times when people
are fearful and dealing with life and death issues. She is mythically
available to return to earth to accompany people as they make
transitions.

Uncovering female figures in the Bible and building meaning
and spiritual resonance for them is essential to creating full equality
for women in Judaism. This requires a conscious and creative artic-
ulation of the tensions of modern Jewish women spoken through
the metaphors and literary forms of prior eras such as *midrash* (tex-
tual exegesis) and *agadah* (storytelling). It also calls for the invigo-
ration of new forms of Jewish expression in the arts, including
dance and drama.

Let me offer some examples. The biblical prophetess Miriam
is now evoked in many contexts, helping to uncover old interpreta-
tions, grafting on new ones. Debbie Friedman, a popular Jewish
folk singer, has written songs about her. The *Midrash* speaks of
Miriam's well, which miraculously followed the Jews during their
years in the desert and provided fresh, healing water. Miriam's
cup, filled with water at the seder table, has been popularized by
feminist seders. She is raised up as Moses' equal as exemplified
by the title of a recent woman's commentary on the Torah, the
Five Books of Miriam, in contrast to the traditional title, the Five
Books of Moses.

Miriam rejoiced with women as the Jews arrive safely at the

other side of the Red Sea. Invoking such a joyous figure can be powerful and wonderful. It is especially important because Miriam was in part vilified by the rabbis. One of our lasting impressions of Miriam, as recorded by the rabbis, is not the rejoicing prophet whose prophecy has been fulfilled, but rather a gossiper whom God condemns with leprosy for speaking behind Moses' back. The rabbis then have used her as a mythic model to promote a stereotype of gossiping, nonintellectual women. Not only do we need to claim Miriam as a positive role model, but we also need to address the ways in which sexism often maligns female characters in the Bible.

The character of Sarah is also a focus for renewed interpretation. Many have added her name alongside the patriarchs in Jewish prayers. Her role as a matriarch reveals a woman of renowned beauty and strength who was also a teacher. Her life with Abraham is now tapped as a paradigmatic source for learning about human relationships. A women's theater group in Jerusalem led by Gaby Lev produced a play based on *midrash* and *agadah* dealing with Sarah's character and her role in the *Akedah*, the attempted sacrifice of her son Isaac by Abraham. The relationship between Sarah and Hagar is studied, critiqued, and interpreted to help us learn how we can create better relationships between Jews and Arabs. The rape of Dina is also brought forth as a story that forces us to acknowledge and redress violence against women internal to our tradition and our peoplehood.

Feminine aspects of God and diverse names of God are now given new prominence in prayer, most notably *Shechina*, the Indwelling of God. Enlarging and diversifying our names for God opens up new paths for relating to God. As long as God is referred to largely as Father and Master, we limit our ability to explore the wealth of spiritual paths in our traditions.

Numerous books are being published to teach more about prominent and everyday women in different periods of Jewish history, from Gluckel of Hameln, a seventeenth-century German-Jewish businesswoman and mother, to Marion Kaplan's work on the lives of German-Jewish women during the Holocaust. Our peoplehood is planted in the study of our texts and a consciousness of our history. As women gain stature and character in society and seek to find themselves in Judaism, this development is crucial. Even the Talmud—a bastion of male rabbinic tradition and a corpus made up of the legal discussions and parables of men from the second to fifth centuries—is now read and written about by scholarly women, specifically with the aim of applying feminist sensibilities to the texts. (See *Rereading the Rabbis: A Woman's Voice* by Judith Hauptman, for instance.)

This explosion of new writing in the past few years has produced ample material for a growing and flourishing Jewish feminist sensibility. In Orthodoxy, where women clearly have a separate and unequal role from men, the International Conference on Feminism and Orthodoxy, chaired by Blu Greenberg, attracted 2,000 participants to its second meeting in 1998.

As Jewish women engage in dynamic ways with our traditional stories and legal texts, we begin to be full owners and inheritors of our tradition. Thus, we become matriarchs of Judaism.

I was asked a few years ago by a Jewish women's project to teach a traditional text on mother-daughter relationships. There was one problem: The existing texts on this subject are not only very rare, but when they do appear they are highly problematic. For example, one rabbinic story explains that Dina was raped because she, like her mother Leah, was a harlot who chased after a man. It is likewise unfathomable, given the wealth of lore and law, that there is no record or expanded tradition of stories about the relationship between Yocheved, Moses' mother, and her daughter, the prophet Miriam. There is a startling absence of any written tradition regarding the relationship between mothers and daughters.

So I took a Talmud text that does deal with an interaction between a mother and a child, presumably a son, to see what we could learn from it if we understand the child to be any child. The narrative I chose deals with how to tell the difference between a young child and an older child. The rabbis bring up a compelling scene: Children wake up in the night and cry out for their mothers. One rabbi claims that this is enough to put a boy or girl in the category of younger child. But another answers that even adults at times cry out in their sleep for their mother. A third rabbi resolves the conflict by saying that if the child cries out "Mommy" once and then stops, she is more mature. If the child cries out Mommy repeatedly, then she is still a youngster.

As the voices of my students filled the room while we discussed this, the text was no longer simply the words of ancient men. It was now filled with the insights, critiques, and additions of masterful women. When the text regains life through animated debate, new understandings are found and women become whole in the tradition.

We must open up the floodgates of women's expression in Judaism. It is through giving voice to the silences that women create space and authority in our community. What persists and is codified and is accepted by communities will by definition be authentic.

Creating New Rituals Sparks Spirituality

A Jewish month begins with the appearance of the new moon. Celebrating this moment—the moment when the cycle begins again, when there is a glimpse of renewal—marks the beginning of a revival of Jewish women's spirituality and ritual. Jewish lore relates that *Rosh Chodesh,* the beginning of a month marked by a new moon, was given to women as a holiday, a reward for not supporting the idolatrous construction of the golden calf. In the past two decades groups of Jewish women have reclaimed this inheritance; in some communities, they have brought back an awareness of *Rosh Chodesh* that had otherwise vanished.

Rosh Chodesh is a moment of hopefulness. In the midst of darkness, groups of women gather together, light candles, refrain from hard work, and share stories, wisdom, and songs. In reclaiming this holiday, which has been overlooked by generations of Jews, Jewish women regain old and new elements of Jewish life. No longer willing to simply take the back seat in the communal religious sphere, women have been challenging the existing tradition and beliefs, and investing their time to develop relevant communal rituals. This is more than simply inserting women into the male patterns; women are renewing and reframing celebrations so they resonate with a range of women's experiences.

There are events and times in our lives that remain uncharted. One interpretation of the creation of the world found in Jewish tradition is that when God created humanity it was an act of separation. To make space in the universe, God had to retreat and allow for distinction. There was a moment in my life when this normally elusive image became very concrete: While giving birth, I suddenly understood what these words meant. For a moment, I sat on God's throne and felt the emergence of a new life, separating from me, becoming distinct, and breathing on his own. How absurd that Jewish tradition has absolutely no rituals for marking this moment of becoming a mother. In addition to creating new rituals, there are many people today involved in bringing new meaning and expression to rituals that already exist but have lost relevance.

The *brit mila,* or circumcision, ceremony can be a passionate drama of gratitude, praise, and commitment. However, it is awkward for Jews who question the need to hurt their infant child with a circumcision. In addition, the liturgy of *brit mila* completely excludes the mother as it invokes the covenant between Abraham and God. By excluding infant girls, *brit mila* evokes a world where girls and women stand outside of active religious life and community. The central binding moment of our religion, then, is between God and men. We must ask ourselves: How can we begin to re-envision this ceremony in a way that makes women full partners in life and speaks to the egalitarian perspective of modern men and women? The physical marking of the body by removing the foreskin is a sign of belonging to a people and commitment to seeking God. Recently, ceremonies marking the birth of baby girls have become very popular and the many practices being used range from washing babies' feet as a ceremony of welcome to offering blessings and prayers. Covenantal ceremonies for girls, however, often lack the focus and intensity of the covenantal transformation bestowed upon boys.

If we choose to keep the rite of circumcision, we must make it more inclusive and consequently meaningful. One easy first step: revising the Hebrew and English liturgy to include the mother in the obligation to perform this rite. The synthesis of spiritual commitment and bodily change recalls generations of male Jews, each adapting to a new world yet celebrating this ancient rite. The act becomes metaphoric as well as physical and brings in the whole community when we add this verse from Deuteronomy: "And the Lord your God will circumcise your heart and the heart of your seed, to love the Lord your God with all your heart, and with all your soul, that you may live." (Deuteronomy 30:6)

The powerful physical experience of giving birth is unattainable (as of yet) by men. However, as female bodies are stretched and maybe torn by bearing life, men's bodies also have been cut, hurt in the intimate place of reproduction and physical ecstasy by circumcision. In this way, the father becomes connected to the physical pain of birth and future sexuality of the child. And yet, in the ritual life of our people, women's experience of birthing is largely ignored and not marked by liturgy or ritual acts to highlight the meaning and spiritual power of the transformative moment. We must enhance our rituals and create new ones.

During the delivery of our son, my partner sang what we termed "our birthing song": a Jewish melody, deeply resonant and joyous. The repeated words were taken from a poem we sing on Friday evenings to welcome the Sabbath, *"ki ba moed,"* which means "the time for rejoicing has come." The same song filled the room at the circumcision, a whole community singing now, and joining the two occasions. We were remaking the tradition to speak to both our experiences and to answer to the morality of our generation. Individualized practices like this are increasingly being created as committed Jews seek personal meaning in intimate life moments. It is this kind of practice that renews Jewish tradition and will transform Jewish spiritual life.

Another example of this is a reworking of *Pidyon haBen,* the Redemption of the First Born. The biblical text, "YHWH spoke to

Moses, saying: Hallow to me every firstborn, breacher of every womb among the Children of Israel, of man or of beast, it is mine" (Exodus 13:1–2), is interpreted to mean that every first-born Jewish son must be redeemed from God. Thirty days after the birth of a first male child, it is traditional to bring the child to a Cohen and buy the infant back from the priesthood. The rabbis, authors of extensive ritual observance, went through millennia of not canonizing a ritual that could incorporate the woman's experience and the existence of first-born infant girls.

The biblical source, however, speaks to the possibility for the mothers, the womb carriers, to mark the physical transition of giving birth for the first time and for infant girls to be included in a ceremony focused on the moment of their entry into the world. The Hebrew phrase, *petter rechem,* "the breacher of the womb," evokes images of the mother's womb being torn open and the experience of the infant setting out on the journey of life. This is just the sort of caveat in the tradition that women have begun to explore for spiritual experiences that can add meaning to life.

On the thirtieth day after my child's birth, eight women friends gathered with me in a circle in a glade of pines. The air was hot and sunny and the baby, swaddled in cloth, lay contentedly asleep in the middle of the group. My body was still bulky and cumbersome, my breasts swollen with milk. The group began to sing to the child and to each other. We spoke of openings and beginnings, and the pain that can accompany creation. The experience of birthing was a personal, private journey. It was now time to enter back into the communal world of adult friends. Each woman gave the baby a blessing, charging him to indeed serve God as well as humanity.

Women can embrace our role as a blessing and welcome the

blessings we can bring forth. No longer silent womb bearers, we claim our places as human beings created and creating in the image of God. In that moment, the fears of bringing a child into a dangerous world, of physical pain and recovery, are comforted by the strength of community. We pray to the ultimate Source of Life and celebrate the joy and responsibility of bearing children. New life emerging from our bodies evokes our partnership with God in the ongoing creation. New rituals grafted onto ancient limbs, for personal moments and also in community, inspire a more meaningful Judaism. They allow for the integration of women's experience of life into a tradition historically recorded and narrated by men, and create a new relationship between us and the natural world.

Reconnecting with the Natural World Creates Spiritual Richness

The majority of American Jews live in large urban centers. However, the *Mishnah,* one of the foundational works of Judaism, is based on an agrarian culture. Many other texts like Psalms and Song of Songs draw on the beauty of nature. How can our agrarian roots along with our appreciation of natural beauty and our awe of God as Creator of the natural world be used to promote and foster Jewish spiritual richness and environmentalism?

To meet the needs of Jews today, our congregations must create new initiatives to reconnect Jews and Judaism with the natural world. This is happening in the form of retreat centers, such as Elat Chayyim, which creates retreats where Jews experience silence in nature and nature-based meditation, learning and spiritual exploration, and the Coalition on the Environment and Jewish Life (COEJL). COEJL helps create and develop community-based

Jewish environmental education, action, and advocacy with annual conferences, campaigns around specific environmental issues, and training seminars for Jewish communal professionals to better use Jewish environmental resources.

Yet much remains to be done to connect the beauty of the natural world described in our prayers and psalms to people's day-to-day experiences. The power of prayer is real when a description of a flower evokes for the person praying an experiential moment in which one takes in with awe the delicate form and color of a flower. Prayer gives that awe new depth by associating it with a Creative God.

To speak relevantly to people today, Judaism must teach that part of our covenant with God is to protect and cultivate the natural world. Our role of stewardship in the natural world is in dynamic tension with our complex relationship of dependance on nature. The applications of how our texts and rituals speak at this level of engagement is only beginning to be explored in the *eco-kashrut* movement and among those who are environmentally concerned. Eco-kashrut calls for rabbinic principles of not hurting animals, and social justice to be applied to our eating and buying practices as committed Jews. Examples of this include not eating veal, only eating free-range chickens and eggs, and not buying products manufactured in countries where child labor is used or there are other human rights injustices.

Over the past decade, I have been involved in a *havura* that explores Judaism in an agrarian context. A *havura* is a circle of Jews that comes together to create a prayer community. Around the country for the last thirty years, small groups have created their own prayer services and communal structures. These have been a tremendously fertile breeding ground for liturgical and spiritual development. In our case, a group of friends began to gather at the farm house where I grew up for the celebration of Shavuot (the Festival of Weeks) and Sukkot (the Festival of Tabernacles). It was no coincidence that these were pilgrimage holidays in ancient Israel. We stage our own pilgrimage to nature and retreat to an environment where we can freely experiment and play, and find meaning as egalitarian, committed Jews.

Shavuot is overlooked by much of the Jewish world because it often occurs just after synagogues have switched to their summer schedules. The synagogue takes a back seat to the season as congregants enjoy more leisure. In the life of more observant Jews, Shavuot is a peak moment in the year when Jews celebrate receiving the Torah on Mount Sinai. Shavuot, however, is also one of three pilgrimage holidays when the early Hebrews went to the Temple in Jerusalem to offer thanks, carrying their first harvest of the year, ripe fruits, and fresh bread. The holiday, then, celebrates the receiving of the law from God and the successful harvesting of food for sustenance. A key feature of it is a full night of communal study punctuated by prayers at dawn. This is the marriage of the Jewish people to God with revelation.

Sukkot, an eight-day autumn holiday, was, like Shavuot, once celebrated by a pilgrimage to the city of Jerusalem. Today, we re-enact the pilgrimage by constructing temporary structures in which to live and eat and by gathering together four types of plants and using them in prayer to evoke the sacrifices. By living outdoors, we place ourselves in God's protection. Of all the holidays, this is the one that seemed most misplaced to me when I lived in a city; now it flourishes in our rural setting. Not only is there the reality of the final harvest of squash, pumpkins, onions, potatoes, and corn, but it is the time of year when we can appreciate living in a temporary dwelling. Some nights are clear and beautiful and others are cloudy or rainy; one is exposed to the elements at their best— and their worst.

In our *havura,* the Sukkot pilgrimage consists of immersing ourselves in rural life, and finding ways to renew traditions for celebration, prayer, and observance. At times, corn stalks, gourds, golden rod, and asters replace the traditional palm, willow, citron, and myrtle as the four types of plants. The brook in the woods becomes a site for ritual immersion. A *mikveh,* or ritual bath, is the traditional way Jews cleanse their spiritual selves. For a woman, the rabbis teach that a *mikveh* is necessary after the conclusion of a menstrual cycle before resuming sexual relations with her husband. For a man, a *mikveh* is no longer directly related to sexual activity but is a way to gain spiritual purity prior to Yom Kippur or weekly before Shabbat. These are ways to be open to the natural world, and to cleanse ourselves of the weight of our daily lives while fulfilling a traditional act.

At our brook in the woods, we all serve as the "*mikveh* lady," a job usually filled by an Orthodox woman wearing a long sleeved dress and a head covering, as we pronounce each other pure at the moment we emerge from the clear, icy water. For women to claim this naked purity as our own, not necessarily related to men or shared sexual lives, is very powerful. How better to ready ourselves to receive Torah, or to stand near God's presence? We sing out the Hebrew words "*kasher, kasher*" and mark the moment of transformation in the midst of an American landscape. Words that have marked millennia of civilization now find their way to a woods that has witnessed only a moment of humanity's journey. The dissonance is startling and pleasing, making us aware of our vital connection to the world we inhabit. Our splashes and songs integrate with the grain of the bark of the trees and the infinity of green leaves; there is a link established between the human history of pilgrimages in honor of God in the ancient cities of Israel and our place in the eternity of natural creation.

Community helps us enter time, in terms of life cycle rituals, but it also helps us leave time and create sacred time, a moment of eternity when historical time does not exist. The ahistorical nature of religious ritual can be a sort of time machine back to Sinai, and even back to Eden.

The holidays of Sukkot and Shavuot occur at the full moon in the lunar cycle. Each time, at the end of a long weekend spent in prayer, song, feasting, study, and play, we gather in a circle in the moonlight. This is a very different experience than the celebration of the New Moon, which welcomes the emergence of light, and daring to go forward. Within these full moon circles of tightly knit friends is the bursting ripeness of life and our love for each other. We are joined by the generations of Jews whose prayers, teaching, songs, and recipes have brought us to this moment of fullness as we stand far from the noise of city life, alone in nature. In these contexts, we can begin to break through to a religion that truly engages the spiritual lives of men and women today.

We Need to Focus Outwardly on Social Issues

Expressions of feminism, personalized ritual, and environmentalism all have to do with finding relevant meaning in an ancient tradition by involving ourselves in the process of change. Living a religious life in Judaism is not just about attending services. These changes all focus on the internal life of individuals in communities. In the past fifteen years, Jews have focused predominantly inward as a people. We have been caught up in our internal struggles over the status of women, the role of Israel, and the struggles between our different movements over "who is a Jew" and intermarriage. We have been less involved with social issues in the greater society.

A primary teaching of Judaism is our responsibility to other people. We need to be engaged in finding meaningful ways to contribute to the world. We need to respond to the growing gap between the poor and the wealthy in our society. Just as prayer can give a context for the experience of awe in nature, religious practice gives a greater structure for us to engage in social justice. Whereas in Orthodoxy this caring usually only extends to fellow Jews, Reform, Reconstructionist, and Conservative Judaism have made clear our responsibility to all parts of society and to other countries. Judaism should not only promote social responsibility but provide a forum in which to sharpen our response to the injustices that surround us. We need effective ways to respond to the homeless, to widespread illiteracy, to racism, and to growing numbers of people without health insurance.

Thankfully, a wave of volunteerism has hit America. Hundreds of thousands, if not millions, of Americans are volunteering. Volunteer service is a tremendous opportunity for community building and finding meaning in day-to-day life. Hands-on work with real people can serve to counteract the emptiness of materialism and give meaning to existence. As the early builders of Israel knew, working together forges bonds between people and affirms values and beliefs. This might mean visiting a sick person, helping create a food pantry, or assisting in the acculturation of a newly immigrated family. But charitable donation has become the predominant way that many Jews help others. Service is no longer as revered by the community as it used to be. In fact, often Jews who work in communal service or teach in religious schools are under-paid and are less valued by the community than those working on Wall Street or in Silicon Valley. To create a community that takes care of itself and of others takes not only full-time professionals but everyone contributing their unique skills.

In the past few years, a number of new programs have sprung up to address the deficit of meaningful Jewish service opportunities. These include: Avodah: The Jewish Service Corps, a program in which young adults spend a year combining Jewish study and communal living with full-time jobs at nonprofit organizations that combat urban poverty; The National Jewish Coalition for Literacy, which mobilizes Jewish volunteers to support existing literacy programs; and the Jewish Organizing Initiative, which integrates a year of working and training in community organizing with Jewish learning. These programs are the first step in what could become a rededication of Jews to community service.

Jewish survival does not lie solely in the pages of ancient texts. It must be engaged with postmodern life and invigorated with new expressions and understandings of Jewish traditions. Only by bringing our current experiences to the table with Jewish history and wisdom will the traditions be nourished and remain vital and compelling for future generations. Uncovering and expanding the voices of women in our ancient texts and writing new texts, creating rituals that enrich and deepen women's and men's lives, sustaining and being sustained by the natural world, and engaging in repairing the world are all ways to make our lives meaningful while drawing on the wells of meaning provided by Jewish culture and history. It is our task to ensure that Judaism is not only fulfilling for the individual but carries humanity one step further in becoming truly humane, ethical, and inspired.

For More Information

Ma'yan, The Jewish Women's
   Project of the JCC on the
   Upper West Side
15 West 65th Street
New York, NY 10023
Tel: (212) 580-0099

Jewish Orthodox Feminist
   Alliance
459 Columbus Avenue, Suite 329
New York, NY 10024
Tel: (212) 752-7133
Fax: (212) 753-6054
E-mail: jofa@rcn.com

Elat Chayyim
99 Mill Hook Road
Accord, NY 12404
Tel: (914) 626-0157

COEJL: Coalition of the
   Environment and Jewish Life
443 Park Avenue South
New York, NY 10016
Tel: (212) 684-6950
E-mail: coejl@aol.com
Website: www.jtsa.edu/org/coejl

National Havurah Committee
7318 Germantown Avenue
Philadelphia, PA 19119
Tel: (215) 248-9760

Avodah: The Jewish Service
   Corps
443 Park Avenue South, 11th
   Floor
New York, NY 10016
E-mail: info@avodah.net
Website: www.avodah.net

National Jewish Coalition for
   Literacy
15 East 26th Street, #1039
New York, NY 10010
Tel: (212) 545-9215
E-mail: njcl@jon.cjfny.org

Jewish Organizing Initiative
94 Forest Hills Street
Jamaica Plain, MA 02130
Tel: (617) 522-3635

THE CHURCH AS A COMMUNITY OF DIALOGUE

Reverend Father Greg Kimura

I am Yonsei, a fourth-generation American of Japanese ancestry.

I am also a fourth-generation Alaskan. My great-grandfather immigrated to the U.S., working his way up the West Coast as a cook, until he ended up in Anchorage in 1918. Anchorage was then a rough place, peopled by laborers, trappers, and gold miners.

The family was interned during World War II as were all Japanese-Americans living along the West Coast. My grandparents met and married in such a camp and my father was born there.

My parents met in college and moved back to Alaska. Father is a postmaster, Mother teaches elementary school.

I grew up the oldest of four boys in the town where I am now a minister—Eagle River-Chugiak, which is now a suburb of Anchorage.

I was raised as a nominal Episcopalian. At Marquette University,
where I was a pre-med major, I carried around a copy of Being and
Nothingness *and avoided the priests on campus. But we were required to*
take a theology class to graduate. There, I was introduced to critical theo-
logical scholarship and philosophy of religion and discovered that many of
the same problems I had with organized Christianity were being tackled
by theologians. My reading turned from chemistry and Sartre to
Bultmann and Tillich.

I changed majors and joined the Episcopal church near school. In
place of the simple worship my parents dragged me to as a child, I experi-
enced incense, chanting, and "church aerobics" (nod, bow, genuflect, stand,
sit, kneel). I was hooked.

After graduating with majors in theology and philosophy, I went
to Harvard Divinity School, which was nondenominational and had
students from every religion. The diversity made for fascinating discussion
and learning. I took an internship at The Church of St. John the Evangelist,
Boston's progressive Anglo-Catholic parish. It has an active ministry to the
poor and a large percentage of gay and lesbian congregants. Sunday ser-
vices were like an Italian funeral: long processions of acolytes, plumes of
heavy incense, and lots of crossing yourself. I loved it.

I graduated in 1993. My thesis, "God and 'Mu': A Prologue to Zen-Christian Theology," analyzed how the Christian idea of God and the Buddhist idea of nothingness operate similarly as limiting concepts in their respective theological systems.

I moved back to Anchorage, where for canonical reasons I had to wait for a year to be ordained. During that time, I was a reporter for the Anchorage Daily News, *where I focused on religion and social issues.*

After ordination, I was called to Holy Spirit Episcopal Church Mission in Eagle River. I have been priest there for five years. Once a month, I serve St. Peter's Episcopal Church in Seward, a rural fishing town two hours to the south. I also regularly serve Christ Church in Anvik, a village in bush Alaska.

When I have time, I read and write. I'm working on a short story based on an experience I had with the village ghost last time I was in Anvik. Like every reporter (or former reporter), I'm working on the Great American Novel that never seems to get done.

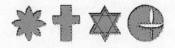

Now as he was going along and approaching Damascus, suddenly a light from heaven flashed around him. He fell to the ground and heard a voice saying to him, "Saul, Saul, why do you persecute me?" He asked, "Who are you, Lord?" The reply came, "I am Jesus, whom you are persecuting. But get up and enter the city, and you will be told what you are to do."

(Acts 9:3–6)

My family became Christian by accident. It happened behind the barbed wire of a Japanese-American internment camp.

It was World War II and Americans of Japanese descent were forced from their homes on the West Coast into internment camps east of the Rockies. In such a camp my grandparents met and fell in love.

Grandfather William was a *Kibei,* born in the U.S. but educated as a young child in Japan. He was an art college student in Seattle before the events following Pearl Harbor changed his life. Grandmother Minnie was a *Nisei,* a second-generation U.S. citizen. She grew up in the small fishing village of Cordova, Alaska, where she worked in her father's laundry.

A Christian pastor agreed to do the wedding. He sympathized with the outcast Japanese-Americans, many of whom lost their homes and belongings as well as their personal liberty. After the service, Grandfather handed him an envelope. It contained four months of wages saved from picking produce on land surrounding the camp.

The pastor handed back the envelope without opening it.

This presented a dilemma for my grandparents. They were raised with a Japanese sense of honor and propriety—what T V shows call "keeping face." They appreciated the pastor's solidarity with internees and his generous rejection of payment. But his action left them without a way to "keep face." Not knowing how else to show gratitude, they converted to Christianity. Grandfather told me they did so out of "a Zen sense of obligation."

I remember when I first heard this story. It was the summer before I entered divinity school to become an Episcopal priest. *This is not how it is supposed to happen*, I thought. *Where was the bolt of lightning? Where was the booming voice from heaven? The personal call? It's supposed to happen like it did to Saul—the notorious persecutor of Christians who, after his conversion, came to be known as St. Paul—on the road to Damascus.*

Instead I find out that my grandparents converted to Christianity because they were good Buddhists?

Looking back on the story, I chuckle. Certainly, it personalizes the common experience of disparity between the way we think things happen—or want them to—in the church and the way they really do.

Rather than resembling St. Paul, my family's conversion seems to have more in common with the legend of the conquered Saxon warriors who were driven by Christian soldiers into a river to drown. Unknown to them, a bishop stood upstream blessing the water. That way they would at least meet their maker baptized in the faith. (No doubt a consolation to the victors rather than the pagan vanquished.)

On a deeper level, the story of my family's conversion personalizes the complexities when different religious and cultural traditions intersect. Misunderstanding, insensitivity, and the experience of simply *talking past each other* too often mark such interactions. The results range from the absurd (my family) to the violent (Saxon warriors).

I'm not sure the church is much better at handling diversity today. But it will have to be. The world we are entering will provide *more* interaction with a *greater* variety of people from *different* backgrounds than ever before. Part of this is due to increased travel, immigration, and trade. Part is due to technological advances, such as the Internet, which provide instant communication around the world.

The net effect is that the world is growing smaller and more connected. As it does, we will have more opportunities to encounter humanity—in all its varied religious flavors—than ever before.

It is essential that people who identify themselves by their faith—as well as their religious institutions—plan thoughtfully for this world. On the eve of the third millennium, we hear reports almost daily about the preparations of end-of-the-world groups. We hear every day of the hysteria surrounding the Y2K problem, which has spawned a type of secular millennialism, but I'm more interested in responsible discussion about the role of the church after the year 2000. How will it need to adapt to its changing environment? What will be the major problems facing it? What will be the new frontiers for ministry and growth?

Of course, the future of the church in an increasingly multireligious environment is not just an issue for mainline Christianity.

All indications are that the U.S. will grow even more diverse. Other important spheres of life, especially the secular and political, are struggling with the coming change.

A constellation of recent debates—from immigration policy to English as our official language to affirmative action—show how divisive the problem of diversity is.

Even a new lexicon of diversity has arisen in the past few years. Terms such as "multiculturalism" and "political correctness" have entered the public domain and become slogans or epithets, depending upon which side you take.

The difference is that, for the church, dealing with diversity is more than a matter of social expedience or political mandate. We are called by God to love our neighbor as ourselves. The fact is that our neighbors are increasingly as likely to be Buddhist, Muslim, Hindu, or atheist, as they are to be Christian or Jewish.

Diversity is a faith issue. And that means it's a theological issue. It cuts to the core of how we in the church think of ourselves as a religion-identified people. It cuts to the core of how we think about God. From the perspective of faith, diversity has very deep implications. Therefore, Christians should have a built-in aversion to the surface treatment that diversity often receives in the secular and political worlds.

From the perspective of the church, diversity and all its allied issues are tied to a way of thinking and a mode of being that claim to run very deep—deeper even than the moral or political dimensions of life. Why? Because diversity impacts the lived experience of the religious person. It describes the context for those endeavoring to live a life of authenticity, justice, and love with other people, the world, and God.

Seen in this context, attitudes toward diversity such as

"respect" and "understanding" are matters of utmost importance. In church-speak, they are matters of "salvation."

We are commanded, as individuals and churches, to take a moral inventory of how we're doing with respect to diversity, and do better. And we believe that our action or inaction is something for which ultimately we will be judged.

This attitude toward responsibility is something I imagine every Christian, from fundamentalist to progressive, can agree on, although maybe they can't agree on how that belief is lived out. And whereas a respectful and sensitive disposition toward others and their religions should always have been the case, it will become a practical necessity in the next millennium.

Why? Because with the increasing diversity comes a new reality for the church.

Increasingly in the future, our accountability will be not only to God, but for our self-preservation. If the church wants to live in a multireligious world, it must adapt. It can continue to cut itself off from the problems of the changing world and insulate itself from diversity. But it does this only at its own peril. People vote with their feet, and the decades-long trend of declining membership in the mainline Protestant churches is evidence.

Furthermore, the church's tendency to separate itself from the changing world is dangerous, especially in the coming age of diversity. Bosnia has become the emblem for religions that not only refuse to speak to each other, but also refuse to live together. While this example is extreme and difficult to conceive in the North American context, does anyone doubt the fervor of religious conviction from every direction on issues such as reproductive choice and gay rights on our soil? Or the violence that percolates up from such fervor?

Again, the question is: Which direction will the church choose to take in a world where increasing diversity is a portent of increasing disagreement?

Will the church entrench itself as one voice among many that are claiming the same thing? That we alone hold the truth on any particular issue? That we can yell louder than anyone else in the cacophony? If we do, the church is both victim and perpetrator of the balkanization of public discourse. If we do, the popular image of the church as anachronism will win in the third millennium.

The Church Must Take a Leadership Role to Provide a New Type of Mission to the World

The history of the mainline Protestant churches (Episcopalian, Presbyterian, United Methodist, Lutheran, and the like) has too often been to play catch-up on the most important issues of the day. Now, as the world enters a time of never-before-seen diversity, it has the potential to lead the world to be a more humane place.

In fact, the church may be one of the few institutions that can do this. It has an abundance of resources that the secular community does not possess with which to deal with the dynamics of the changing world. The church is a ready-made community of fellowship: It is voluntary, it meets regularly (at least once a week), and members potentially belong to it for their entire lives.

In most cases, church and denomination are the same across generations and extended relatives in a family. Church members enjoy a stability that is rare in today's world and that will probably be rarer in the future. People are mobile. They relocate for work. They change neighborhoods. They buy new houses. Wherever they go, if the church of their upbringing is a tradition like Presbyterian, Methodist, Episcopal, and so forth, they can find a parish that connects them with their family and their past.

The church contains within its membership much of the social and economic diversity of the world, especially on the regional and denominational level. In the case of my own communion, the figures of Desmond Tutu and George Bush come to mind. On opposite ends of the spectrum in almost every sense, they at least hold a common form of prayer book worship and Anglican spirituality.

Even though my own parish is largely middle-class, there is a wide range of people—white, black, Asian, and Native. The largest and fastest-growing group in the church consists of members of the armed services. (This is a bit odd for me, since I am a dyed-in-the-wool liberal.) Being a member of my parish, let alone its pastor, I am confronted with a diversity of people that I would not normally be in contact with in the secular world.

The Episcopal Church of today is not the Virginia planter and Boston Brahmin church of earlier eras. It is certainly not "the Republican Party at prayer," as it was once known. The truth of the matter is that the membership of all the mainline Protestant denominations is in flux and already contains much of the diversity that exists in the world. The goal should be to expand the circle.

The greatest strength the church holds is its voice. It can speak with credibility and authority on matters of social concern. It has an organization and structure that is both grassroots (the parish) and international (the Church).

The church enjoys a fund of stories (Bible) read corporately every week. These tell how, in the distant past, God helped people adapt to change in ways that are humane and godly. These stories continue to fire the spiritual imagination of people. Who can imagine the civil rights movement, the most important social movement of our time, without the inspiration of Exodus and the Gospel?

The reason these stories hold such power is that they are not "Ragged Dick" and they are not a "Book of Virtues." They are not easy tales with a convenient moral. The majority of Bible stories teach about people's abject failure in living lives of sustained faith.

The Gospels—the part of the New Testament that tells of Jesus' life—spend a few chapters (in the case of Mark and John, none at all) speaking of Jesus' birth and about Christ's rising from his grave on Easter. The rest are a lengthy spiritual biography of Jesus and his disciples, where Jesus repeatedly teaches and the people repeatedly misunderstand. Eventually, even his closest followers turn away from him and let him be crucified and killed.

Out of these narratives of tragedy, the church preaches a message of reconciliation and repentance, of struggle, failure, and hope. This is not a sentimental message or a naive hope. It preaches that life is riven with ambiguity and failure, yet also full of redemptive love. And the church's people believe that, just as God aided the faithful in the past, God similarly acts in the lives of people in the present.

Community. Voice. Stories. These are powerful resources the church can bring to the postmodern world. It can utilize these resources and its institutions to provide a new type of mission to the world.

We Can Become a Community of Dialogue

First, the church should begin to think of itself and its role to the non-church world as a mediator. Institutionally, the church can mediate the problems of a multi-religious society by being a "community of dialogue."

By "community of dialogue," I mean a place that both protects and promotes real, deep dialogue among its members and the outside world. That is, the church should be a safe space—a sanctuary—for diverse groups to speak freely and on the most intimate levels about the issues that affect them.

But a "community of dialogue" is more than just a sanctuary. It is a place that, from time to time, "nudges" its members. It pushes them into dialogue—and thus relationship—with people of different ideas and backgrounds from themselves. Real, deep dialogue sometimes happens when we listen and agree. Sometimes it happens when we listen and vociferously disagree. Real, deep relationships are built when, in spite of those disagreements, we continue to remain in a fellowship of conversation.

Second, the church needs to aggressively adapt itself and its mission to a religiously plural world. Perhaps in the past it has been more known for attracting people of similar background and belief. Martin Luther King, Jr. called 11 A.M. Sunday the most segregated hour of the week. Things have changed, but I'm afraid he would not be encouraged by the situation thirty years later as we prepare for life in the new millennium.

Whatever its failure in the past, the need for a "community of dialogue" is manifest. The secular and political world tend to reward glibness in our communication. The soundbite and e-mail exemplify this reality: Instead of actual dialogue, throw out a pithy slogan; instead of face-to-face interaction, send a message into the nonspatial unreality of cyberspace. Real communication is becoming increasingly efficient. It is also becoming increasingly thin—a double-edged predicament that seems to follow every new technological advance. Yet, it is precisely at this time that our awareness of diversity is the greatest, as well as our need for sustained dialogue.

And if leadership and the exigencies of the faith-life are not

motive enough, the church needs to become a "community of dialogue" to prove its relevance to an increasingly unchurched world.

Generation X—the first generation coming into adulthood in
the new millennium—is the first generation in this country to have
more of its members raised outside of church or synagogue than
within.

They, not the so-called "heathens" of faraway continents, are
the new mission field. The probability is that individual members of
Generation X, born 1964–1980, and Generation Y, born after 1980,
did not go to Sunday school. Therefore, they don't share a background of Bible stories and music. They don't share a religious
vocabulary. They don't share a corporate experience of a community of faith and experience with the positive resources that the
church brings.

In many instances, Gen-Xers don't even assume that church is
important. Surveying the mixed history of the church, they often
see it as an enemy of diversity. They may be interested, at least
superficially, in other religions, but not in the Christian and Jewish
mainline.

We need to win them over but we need to get them through
the doors first. And to do that, we need to give them a reason to
come. The church can do this by becoming a "community of
dialogue."

At the same time it is making converts, the church can renew
itself with a sense of purpose and ministry to a world of diversity.
It can be goal-oriented, not in terms of numbers and growth (when
people in the church speak like census takers you know something
is wrong) but in terms of the quality of social discourse and
relationship. It can be the example of a place where the difficult

problems that come with a world of diversity are meted out. In fact, it can be *the* place where these problems are discussed.

As the church enters the third millennium, it is at a crisis. In the Greek sense of the word, a crisis is a point not only of fear but of possibility. The third millennium is the Rubicon for mainline Christianity and, I might add, for Judaism as well. There's no going back. Either we will become a place that is relevant to the needs of the coming world, or we will continue to decline, fading out, Eliot-like, with a whimper not a bang.

Openness and Dialogue—Not a Community of Faith—Must Characterize the New Church

This is a good news/bad news proposition for the church.

The good news it that to change, it must rediscover a rich part of its heritage. The church was founded on the twin concepts of openness and dialogue. In church-speak, that is one way we define "sanctuary": a sacred safe-house where God, individuals, and the faith-community itself come together; where Christians come to listen and interact, laugh and cry on the most personal levels.

Today, the church must become a postmodern sanctuary. In a world of increasing ethnic, cultural, and ideological diversity, the church must symbolize the one place where differences are truly encouraged.

It must be a haven for those who are struggling to make sense of life in the midst of the rapidly changing world. And it must encourage real dialogue among its different members, especially those who come from non-Western traditions. It must also enter-tain a continuing conversation as to how God—whatever God looks like—fits into things.

The bad news is that to become such a place, the church must give up some ideas that it holds dearly. First is the traditional idea of the community of faith. The church must sacrifice the notion that it is a community defined primarily by creed, confession, and doctrine. The church must understand itself first and foremost to be a sanctuary for free and open dialogue, where people of all stripes seek it out precisely because it is such a place.

From its beginning, the church sought out diversity. St. Paul, the biblical figure with the conversion experience, is also the missionary *par excellence.* His commission was to reach out and spread the Gospel to diverse communities:

> "But the Lord said to him, 'Go, for he [Paul] is an instrument whom I have chosen to bring my name before Gentiles and kings and before the people of Israel . . . "
>
> *(Acts 9:15)*

The word "gentiles" comes from Latin and literally means "those of [other] nations or races." St. Paul, himself a Jew, became "The Apostle to the Gentiles." In the Bible, God explicitly called him to minister to those not like himself.

The church was to be a new type of community—a sanctuary for people of different nationalities and ethnicities. A home where everyone found acceptance as an invaluable soul.

Each person is created by God, therefore each individual is important. This basic attitude was largely responsible for the growth of the church in the first centuries after Jesus' death.

The church was a counterculture to Roman society and Roman religions, many of which limited membership to higher social classes or imposed fees. It also developed a social service network, including primitive hospitals, and emphasized charity and mercy. Recent biblical and archeological research—to the chagrin of some conservative churches—illustrates that women held leadership roles from the earliest times.

This is not to exonerate the church from its less than admirable moments in history. But from its beginning in the ministry of Jesus, the church identified itself with socially outcast people—the diseased, the poor, the disempowered. The best known piece of Christian scripture, the Beatitudes, is itself a paean to the miserable:

> "[Jesus said,] Blessed are the poor . . . those who mourn . . . the meek . . . those who hunger and thirst . . . the merciful . . . the pure in heart . . . the peacemakers . . . those who are persecuted . . . blessed are you when people revile you and persecute you and utter all kinds of evil against you falsely on my account. Rejoice and be glad . . . for in the same way they persecuted the prophets . . . ."
>
> *(Matthew 5:2–12)*

In the Greco-Roman world of Jesus' day, the *paterfamilias* was the dominant model of community. An undemocratic democracy, where power and dignity were limited to property-owning men. Patterning itself on scriptures such as the Beatitudes, the church turned this model on its head and extended the notion of the inclusive community. The beatific model of the church is what kept my grandparents coming to church after their wedding.

The way Grandmother tells the story, after refusing the money, the pastor told them to join a church when they returned home. After the war, Grandfather and Grandmother made their way to Anchorage, where they found a hostile, openly discriminatory community. I have always hesitated asking my grandparents about the early years. Much of what I know is culled from books written by internees returning to areas where there was a sizable Japanese-American community. Anchorage did not have the benefit of such a community and the mutual support it carries.

The Japanese-Americans who did return to Anchorage stood out. They were easy targets for racist attacks. Having spent the war locked up by their own country for crimes they did not commit, they came back to a place that still blamed them for these crimes. It was an awful time, and I know that recalling it, half a century later, still hurts.

During the congressional hearings for reparations, Grandfather and Grandmother both testified. It was the first time I heard them speak about the inhuman treatment in their camp, but also about their travail upon returning to Anchorage. Of finding homes ransacked, and discovering their belongings in their neighbors' houses. Of a business lost. Of a general atmosphere of distrust and the feelings of guilt, even though they had done nothing wrong.

But Grandmother and Grandfather also found the local Episcopal church, and an understanding priest. Their experience of church was the experience of sanctuary from a hostile society, during internment and after.

On the most basic level, church was where they were treated as human by others—where they heard the word spoken and preached that they were human. Church was a place where they could come to lay their burdens on God and work out some of their bitterness with humankind. A place to find solace and strength. A place and a community of acceptance.

This understanding of church as sanctuary preceded any particular doctrine about God. With respect to their initial conversion, it happened in spite of any doctrine about God.

I believe the experience of community of this type is what draws people to church. This is true from St. Paul's time to now. As much as we clerics like to think that it is because of the sermon or the service, it is usually during coffee hour afterward that converts are made.

Nowadays, this is especially true. People want what they are increasingly unable to find in secular life. People speak in sentimental terms of the "loss of community." They are frightened by media stories of senseless violence. They pine for a world of ethical restraint. They seek a place where people respect each other's humanity.

The sense is pervasive that something else has been lost in the progress of twentieth-century America. People express a lack of connection with something that takes them outside of themselves. Even the unchurched feel the need for transcendence. They are so desperate they even seek it where their better sense tells them they won't find it. Tune in to late night television sometime. Every other commercial is for psychics.

The church is the sanctuary for transcendence and it is composed of people who celebrate the sacred. This is what we—what God—has to offer.

What people are attracted to in the church is what they know the church is supposed to be about: real connection with God and with other people. That is why many so-called baby boomers are returning with their own kids to the church that they couldn't get away from fast enough as teenagers.

I overstate the case to make the point. It is not that the church's theology doesn't matter. It is because of the way we think of God that we derive the idea of the church as sanctuary in the first place.

It is because of the way that God is conceived of and described in the peculiarly Christian way that *we* are who we are.

Because God creates us in the divine image, we are worthy of respect. Because God was sacrificed in Christ Jesus, we are redeemed in love. Because the Holy Spirit is with us, we are sustained to love one another, especially in our diversity.

The challenge for the church is to get back to these biblical and theological roots. To attract those who are seeking, the church must see its primary mission as pursuing diversity. Like St. Paul, we need to see this as Christianity's destiny—because it is the world's destiny—and as its strength.

We Must Create Communities Where Diversity Is Welcome

The idea that the church should be a sanctuary for different people is not controversial for Christians. Of course, the goal is to share the Gospel with everyone. To get people reading the Bible. To invite others to connect with God and each other in the church context.

The problem for those who view the idea of the church as a sanctuary for real dialogue from the outside is that the church has not always lived up to that belief. And then the church looks hypocritical. Too often it has followed, rather than led, the trends of the larger society of the last generation. This has been to its detriment.

The mainline Protestant church, for example, has followed its traditional middle-class constituency from the cities to the suburbs. In doing so, it has invested energy and money in the very areas that are most likely to have the least amount of diversity of income, race, and politics.

We have created our churches, if not our God, in the image of the suburbs.

This has been a recipe not only for monotony, but for declining membership. Every mainline Protestant denomination has seen a fall in the past fifty years. Some in absolute numbers, all in percentage of the population.

Even the rise in fundamentalist and evangelical churches, which have already hit their peak, was largely due to shifting membership from the mainlines rather than integrating new and different groups.

The simple fact is that the future church will need to look like the future America if it wants to survive and flourish—and the future America appears to be getting more tan.

For too long we have thought of race and identity in terms of black and white. What is happening now is referred to as the "browning" or "California-izing" of U.S. immigration from Asia, the fastest growing percentage of the population. Also, in many areas of the West, Hispanics are becoming the dominant group in absolute numbers.

The church needs to jump on this trend. It needs to evangelize, first of all by making people feel welcome when they walk through the door of the church. It needs to actively recruit members from these groups when they aren't appearing at the church door.

Since becoming ordained, I have watched with befuddled amazement the same circular debates over church growth each year. The answer is simple to me: If the church wants more Alaska Native members (let alone to keep its present Alaska Native members) or Japanese-American members or fill-in-the-blank members, it needs to ordain more Alaska Natives, Japanese-Americans, and fill-in-the-blanks.

The church needs to take its cue from the best universities in the U.S., which identified the diversity trend long ago. And, though the universities have had their own battles in the multicultural wars, they have also become stronger as a result.

The mainline Protestant church has lost much of its identity by allowing the name "Christian" and words like "traditional" to be co-opted by fundamentalists and evangelicals. This has made possible an equation between the church and particular conservative political agendas. This connection in itself turns unchurched people off to the church.

The picture of Christianity molded by fundamentalists and evangelicals is not salutary in an age of diversity. Their vision harkens back to a time when the concerns of a diverse population were not represented. They even valorize a time when outside groups were not seen as an equal part of the community.

Further, fundamentalist and evangelicals are the least inclined to enter into the type of full dialogue that the church will have to require as we enter the coming millennium (if they think the world will last that long!). The bottom line is they appear to be more interested in monologue than dialogue. They tend to remove themselves from conversation. Their medium is televangelism, where the preacher can preach at you all day long and all you do is listen.

These groups are the modern analog to the conquering Christians: Convert the infidels willingly or drown them in the water of baptism. The end is the same. Such a retrograde vision is opposite the type of sanctuary that Jesus spoke about in the Beatitudes.

Sometimes, I feel like most of what I am doing as an Episcopal priest is working to undo all the bad work and misconceptions that have been largely circulated by fundamental and evangelical churches. But if we take as a given the fact that, beginning with Gen X, we are moving into the most unchurched time in American history, this sort of "reclamation ministry" will be much of the task of the mainline Protestant churches.

A common conversation I have as a university chaplain with incoming students goes something like this:

Me: Why don't you come to Bible study/noonday prayer/serve dinner at the shelter?

Student: I'm not really into religion.

Me: That's what study/prayer/social outreach is about—learning about what it means to pray/discuss scripture/live as a religious person.

Student: I'm into spirituality, not religion.

Me: That's what I'm talking about.

Student: No, I'm not interested in the rules and commandments. I'm a seeker. I'm into the experience. I'm interested in lots of faiths: Buddhist, Celtic, Wiccan, Yoga, Sufi, Rastafarianism . . .

Me: Every faith has rules and commandments.

Student: Maybe. Basically, I'm into anything *but* Christianity.

Then I spend the rest of the semester trying to get the student to at least consider Christianity along with the rest of the faiths.

Christianity is perceived to be intolerant, repressed, hypocritical. Christianity is the Inquisition. Or it's the guy on TV with big hair asking for money one day, then begging for forgiveness the next because he has sinned. Fundamentalists have accomplished the worst thing they could do for ministry to young people: They have made Christianity uncool.

In spite of this, the church must become relevant to Gen X, not by being aggressive but by being an open "community of dialogue."

The young person coming into adulthood, seeking among a variety of religions but with no religious background of his or her own, is precisely the type of person the church needs.

John and Charles Wesley knew that. Their movement, Methodism, barely 150 years old, is now the second largest Protestant denomination in the U.S. Methodism began among restless college students who wanted the authentic, personal religious experience they were not finding in the established church.

The Wesleys understood what the mainline Protestant church must appreciate today: that this type of inquisitiveness and creativity will help the church adapt to life in the new millennium. The question is, how do we create a community of faith that will make postmodern seekers feel welcome?

The church can shrug off the image of stuffiness by becoming a "community of dialogue," a sanctuary for this type of seeking, and a repository for people with different ideas of God. It can replace the *Saturday Night Live* caricature of the Church Lady with the image of Thomas Aquinas, the medieval theologian and seeker who once called himself a "pious agnostic."

By doing this the church would do the universities a service. To my surprise, I discovered as a chaplain that many students do not have even a basic knowledge of important Bible stories—stories that have inspired not only the faith of believers but the arts and humanities for centuries. This is a frustration I have heard expressed more than once by professors who are colleagues of mine. Students may know the story of Christmas because it has almost become a secular holiday, but they don't know the meaning of Easter. Of the great stories from the Hebrew Scriptures, even less can be assumed.

If students do not know these stories, how can they understand the symbolism of Dante or Joyce? How can they appreciate the rage of Nietzsche or the intricacies of Foucault?

The Church Needs to Model Itself on the University to Become a "Community of Dialogue"

The persistent question on the lips of the unchurched is, "Why go to church?" With no such social expectation that they attend, and being inherently skeptical and suspicious of the church, they don't see much reason to go. The current situation resembles more of the church in St. Paul's day than in my grandparents'. It has to seek out converts in a world of tremendous cultural diversity and tailor its institutions to that world. Like the early church, it must reach out to the most needy and vulnerable. But it must also show that it has something to give that cannot be found elsewhere—the sense of depth and of community.

But how can such a sanctuary be formed in a diverse world, when one of the hallmarks of such a world is the feeling that real community is not possible because consensus on any given issue is not possible anymore, especially those that deal with our most profound and persistent problems, such as race, poverty, gender, and lifestyle?

We already have a secular model to follow, one that I suggest we learn from: the university.

I have had the pleasure of spending time pursuing degrees or working at a Jesuit university, an Ivy League university, a state university, and a small, formerly religiously affiliated liberal arts college. Each had a radically different educational philosophy. But they all shared much in common.

Like the church, the university is composed of people from different geographic, ethnic, and ideological backgrounds. Unlike the church, the university does exclude a certain amount of diversity. The uneducated are, by definition, not in college and the truly poor are not either.

At most universities, people spend the first year or two living together in a dormitory. They take many of the same introductory level courses at the beginning but their interests and talents vary and they end up in a variety of academic majors.

The university—or, I should qualify, the *good* university—is an experiment in creating community where people with different backgrounds and deepening academic interests engage each other. It also cultivates dialogue and interaction wherever it can, not only in the classroom, but on the playing field, in the cafeteria, and during late night debates in dorm rooms on life, liberty, and the pursuit of happiness.

The university is sanctuary for free thought and expression and a meeting place for reasoned discussion and inevitable disagreement. It is in constant tension, and the tension breaks out from time to time. But that is the price for having a university community.

Even at the Jesuit school I attended, which took unapologetic stands on issues, the attitude was "anything goes in the classroom." That is what the mainline church should strive to emulate.

The goal of this type of education is intellectual and moral growth through rigorous study and personal interaction. Dialogue—with a text, with peers, and with professors—is the mode of learning. And the value of this type of education is not professional development but character development to pursue a vocation. The university, like the church, is led by higher ideals.

The problem with the university community is that it is not for everybody. It is selective, expensive, and temporary. You are expected to leave it eventually and enter the "real world."

But the church needs to model itself on the university so it can become a "community of dialogue." The church, in fact, is called to be even more open to diversity than the university.

Like the university, the church has the institutional capacity to bring people together to interact on the most personal level. It needs to protect and promote discourse on the important issues of the day, because all of these have theological implications. It should seek to encourage discussion, not simply answer it.

Dialogue versus Dogma

I once gave a talk at the local Unitarian Universalist Fellowship. Afterward, I told one member of the Fellowship that such a series, led by different people every week, was something my own church should consider doing since the Unitarian church was approaching something like a "community of dialogue." (The member said he had once been to an Episcopal church. Unitarians and Episcopalians were just as likely to debate theology, but at least the Episcopalians could agree on hymns!)

The "community of dialogue" that I saw at the UU Fellowship and the university are models for how building such a community might be done; they are not molds. This does not mean that mainline Protestant churches should throw out what makes them mainline—their views on bible, liturgy, creed, confession, and so forth. It also doesn't mean rearranging Sunday morning as a talking circle or twelve-step confessional. It means, at its most basic, a change in attitude. An openness to difference and an encouragement of interaction among that difference.

The UU Fellowship and the University communities are struggling with their own internal tensions in an age of increasing diversity. Unitarian Universalism is among the most highly educated and wealthy denominations in the U.S. It is also largely monocultural. Usually people stay at universities for four years. It is a temporary community, not a lifelong association. The mainline Protestant church does contain a lot of diversity (although it should work for more) and it offers membership that can be lifelong.

Thus the church, as an institution and as a tradition, has tools that are not available to either institutions of higher learning or to less theologically structured denominations such as Unitarian Universalism. We have the potential to show both groups much about real, deep dialogue in a world of diversity. We can also change our idea of community and become a sanctuary for dialogue, instead of our traditional mode of community based on dogma.

Since the age of the Ecumenical Councils in the fourth through the eighth centuries, the church solidified community around the idea of consensus. Consensus in terms of the content of the creeds that came out of those councils that many still recite every Sunday like the pledge of allegiance. The Episcopal church is like that, as are the Roman Catholic, Lutheran, Methodist, and many other churches.

In other Protestant communions, the same idea of community exists, but consensus focuses upon a confessional document that arose from the time of the Protestant Reformation or later. Many Presbyterian churches are like this, as is the largest Protestant denomination, the Southern Baptists.

As the church enters the third millennium, the world has become a place where consensus on the most important issues is not possible. In many cases, it is not even desirable.

Our world looks upon community based upon assent to creed or confession as dangerous or irrelevant and the very future of the church is not at all certain. Yet there is a deep yearning for the spiritual dimension of life. People are fascinated by religion, but repulsed by the doctrine and dogma that seem to go with it. Some want to participate in a community of faith but fear they will not be welcome.

Perhaps they do not understand the doctrine. Perhaps they disagree with particular points. Perhaps they just want to learn.

The type of community that would attract them is one where honest questions and the process of questioning are respected in the search for religious meaning, where the church is a place to find and discover rather than to be told what to do or what to believe.

These seekers would be attracted to a church that sees itself as a sanctuary for ideological diversity.

This does not mean that we give up the beliefs that make us what we are. But engaging members and prospective members in a dialogue about their views on God and church would be mutually beneficial. This would be no-holds-barred and in plain language, not the churchy jargon we often fall into for convenience. It would also help the church understand more of the spiritual needs of the present culture so that it can adapt, as it has in every generation and culture.

Some of the most theological conversations I have ever had are of this type.

I have learned much about God from people who don't consider themselves religious talking about times in their lives when they have had a sense of the divine. Sometimes they look at me furtively, self-conscious that their stories don't involve church. The most important thing is to listen, and to honor the story. The church is at its best when it operates with this sense of openness.

But the world that we are moving into contains much more than ideological diversity. It is composed of different cultures and religions. In the past, the church may have even regarded these groups adversarily. Now, its attitude must change as well.

A Place for Multiple Voices

Whether it is to non-Western heritages and religious traditions, feminism, or ecological consciousness, many people are reaching out to a variety of sources in the search for spiritual meaning. The church not only needs to keep the door open for them but actively embrace them in their search.

I have grown, for instance, by rediscovering Zen philosophy and meditation and finding that, in subtle ways, the faith of my family has always been enriched by its Eastern heritage. By discovering more about myself in Zen, I have become a better Christian. I even think of myself as a combination Zen-Christian Episcopal priest, if such a thing is possible.

I am now in the third generation of my family that is part of the church. The real test of our ability to love our neighbor will be to respect their faith and seek to understand them better without trying to convert them or ignore them, especially when they come from a non-Western background.

In this way, the role of the church should be as a sanctuary for dialogue *among* traditions. Ironic as this sounds, the church is uniquely situated to mediate the diversity of the coming age. First, it has a tradition of openness and dialogue that derives from its inestimable value of the person.

Second, the church is an institution of size, with considerable diversity within itself. For some people, the only place they see, let alone interact with, people from different cultural and socio-economic groups, is in church. Not in every church is this the case, and certain denominations, especially Roman Catholics, are better at this. But here I see a great potential for growth.

Third, the church is intimately concerned with the welfare of the world and the well-being of all people. Conflict that arises from ignorance and misunderstanding between people of any faith—or no faith—is an opportunity for the church to act as reconciler.

If we become the place that brings diverse groups together and keeps them in dialogue, we can show others that the process of dialogue itself is a working of God.

In the best of conversations, we witness something of the holy. The interaction produces a discovery of the other, and a self-discovery. There is revelation and growth in wisdom.

A sense of connection with each other is reinforced in dialogue. That connection makes it difficult to dehumanize the other, which so often leads to lack of understanding and even violence.

The church is called to shepherd the voices within our growing diversity. It has powerful resources of its own to offer as a mediator and it has a tradition of critical discourse. Its members see themselves as responsible to God and to each other and they engage in theological reflection and moral self-inventory.

By asking themselves questions like, "Am I living biblically? What does it mean to live with the Beatific view in today's world?", they are in conversation not just with the present but also in living relationship with stories from the past. By reading, discussing, and inwardly digesting the stories of the Bible and of saints' lives, they are inspired to live in a Godly, humane way.

In the future world of diversity, we can draw on these resources and expand our mission. We will have to give up the idea of ourselves as a "community of creed/confession/doctrine," but, in doing so, we can liberate ourselves from the image of church as being irrelevant today.

The question for the future of the church is not only of its relevance but of its continued existence. We can go the way of the Shakers, or we can reinvent ourselves and our ministry for the new millennium. Sacrificing our previous dogmatism in favor of "dialogue" may be the only way we can remain faithful to Jesus Christ.

MY VISION OF THE NEW SPIRITUAL LIFE IN AMERICA

Roshi Norman Fischer

My initial interest in Zen began during my college days, through my reading and pondering about questions of life and death, questions that were powerfully with me as a child, but that I had put aside during adolescence when other concerns took center stage.

In my twenties, I was looking for a way to understand what was going on, and some books about Zen happened to fall into my hands. They immediately made sense to me.

For a number of years, my Zen practice was quite traditional. I did intensive meditation and text study for a while on my own in the backwoods of northern California, and then later in Zen Mountain Center, the first American Zen monastery founded by Shunryu Suzuki-roshi, in the Los Padres National Forest near Carmel, California. I was ordained as a Zen priest, spent five years in the monastery, then moved to a Zen temple near San Francisco, where I still live.

Traditional Zen practice is quite regimented: predawn wake up, meditation in black robes, Japanese chanting, silent speedy temple cleaning, meal ritual. Eventually I realized that the essential experience of Zen meditation can be achieved without altars and robes, without predawn chanting and monastic ritual. You can just sit on a chair and breathe.

I also realized that meditation isn't just Buddhist or just Zen; that sitting quietly with the mind is a universally relevant experience, and that this can have an effect on work, relationships, health, and general attitudes and approaches to life.

When I began my Zen training, I had never known of Buddhism so it took me a while to get the hang of it: about twenty years. Then it took another ten to give myself permission to be flexible with the tradition. About thirty years to get to the beginning! This is not, of course, the case with Western clergy people who take up traditions that they were born into. They hit the ground running, so to speak, and find new trails more quickly than I did. Although I'm at least middle-aged in life, I'm a baby in the dharma (the Buddhist teaching). That's how it goes.

Religion fascinates me. I am constantly amazed by the various ways that humans go about the impossible task of articulating and developing their inmost feelings about being human. I would rather attend a church service or climb a Mayan temple than attend a baseball game or a concert. For my money, religion has always been less about being good or right, about finding absolute truth, than about exploring what it means to be human and finding a way to live out the implications of the process. I think it is a shame, although it seems quite natural, that religion becomes so culturally determined. When I was young, living in a small town in Pennsylvania, religion was what one received from one's family. It was completely taken for granted, and there was nothing lively or perplexing about it. If your parents were Methodists or Catholics, so were you; and being Methodist or Catholic meant that you sang in this way, went to church in that place, celebrated holidays with this or that set of customs. You were also supposed to believe something in particular, but the truth is that very few people really knew what those beliefs were, and even fewer actually believed them.

This is all right as far as it goes. It is even wonderful as far as it goes. Having a place to worship and a community to worship with, having a set of beliefs to subscribe to or keep at least intact for a sense of certainty about life . . . all this can be comforting, and can provide the context for a good, satisfying life. But—at least as far as I am concerned—it does not go far enough because religion, most deeply understood, is also outside of culture. It occurs at the place where culture, even psychology, ends. I always enjoyed the Jewish background in which I had been brought up and had no quarrel with it. But when I was confronted with the toughest questions of my life—questions of meaning, questions of purpose, life and death questions that arose out of despair and suffering—I knew that I needed experiential spirituality, and it simply did not occur to me to look for that in my Jewish roots. I think that the new spirituality has everything to do with this sort of experiential spiritual exploration.

Religion Must Explore and Care for the Human Heart

Unlike any other discipline I know, the results of our religious exploration are almost indescribable in ordinary language. You can't use math either, and you can't use metaphor, at least not in the usual literary sense. Religious exploration seems to require a specialized language and the cultivation of a set of attitudes, emotions, and practices to go with that language to make it, to some extent at any rate, understandable, suggestible. And so there are religious traditions, each quite different from the other, that provide the context necessary for this deep, essential exploration of the human heart.

It is clear that we need to take care of our bodies with good exercise and diet. It is clear that we need to take care of our minds by reading and studying. It is also clear that our psychological well-being, our emotions, relationships, and our own healthy sense of who we are as personalities, need tending. Doctors, teachers, and therapists help us with all of that. But beyond that is the need to take care of our deepest, most intimate self: The impermanent, shifting, indefinable self that changes, grows old, and dies, but somehow endures; the self that seeks meaning and purpose; the self that is often unknown and alone as it confronts the world. This is the territory that any religion needs to explore today.

Religious Traditions Today

In centuries gone by, I think religious traditions held an almost imperialistic sway over our most intimate life questions. Each religious tradition insisted on the primacy of its own truth to the exclusion of all others, even to the point of being ignorant and scornful of others, as well as of secular ideologies and disciplines. Because of this, the last century or so saw the eclipse of religion. Very few forward-looking people embraced or espoused it. Instead physical and social sciences, the arts, and psychology provided us with all the explanations we thought we needed. The liveliness of our life, we assumed, was there.

Now at the end of the millennium this is no longer the case. It is clear that all the answers we need will not be found in the secular disciplines. We are coming to a realization that religion is necessary, and we have a new sense of what religion is and how it functions in our lives. It is not that religion is the truth, taking precedence over everything else as though it were a cloud that covers the sky of our lives. We are seeing instead that religion is a crucial aspect of who we are as human beings, and that this aspect can be found everywhere in us. It is not more important or more profound. It is simply there and necessary, as everything in our lives is important and necessary.

In addition, we are seeing that the various traditions are not really contending and mutually exclusive truth systems. Traditions are, of course, different from each other. Each has something to offer. Each has advantages and disadvantages. Each can be useful to the person who chooses to use it.

In other words, we now know that religion is for people, not the other way around.

In the last few years, as I have become more flexible with my own tradition, I have come to see that the scriptures, the practices, the customs of any religious tradition all fit together. Many thousands of great minds, over centuries, have worked things out, often through bitter disagreement, eventually smoothing the way so that a religious tradition is something beautiful and whole, in and of itself.

People, on the other hand, are not quite so coherent, and the more we look honestly at ourselves, at our impulses and deepest thoughts and desires, the more contradiction we find. Insofar as we give ourselves more and more permission to be open to what we feel, we find more and more contradiction, more and more complexity.

In my own working with people over the last ten years or so I have seen that the contradictions within people do not always fit the coherence of religious traditions. For many people, a particular tradition may fit quite well in some ways, but in other ways it simply does not, and people sometimes suffer and do violence to their spirits in order to fit themselves into a particular tradition. And sometimes, for some people, one tradition fits in some ways, but another tradition fits in other ways. People experience a lot of pain over this sort of thing: *If I am a good Christian,* they may say, *why do I need to practice Zen? And if I am a good Zen person, why do I feel the need to go to church on Christmas Eve?*

I think we are now just beginning to discover that these contradictions may be all right. Of course, to practice religion we need
to give up preference and go beyond our desire and conditioning,
so it is not the case that anything we want or prefer is always just
fine. We need a sense of renunciation and rigor in our practice,
which is an ongoing committed willingness to go on with something, even if it is sometimes difficult or unsatisfactory.

The New Spirituality Should Be Existentially, Not Culturally, Based

But even with all this, I have found that a certain ecumenical
mixing of traditions is characteristic of the new spirituality. I think,
in particular, of a friend of mine who has been practicing Zen dili-
gently for many years. He has done daily meditation practice and
countless one-day and one-week Zen retreats. He has lived in a
monastery for a training period, has taken ordination, has studied
texts. But little by little over the years, he began to feel that something was missing in Zen for him, that the tradition, while warm
and friendly, was lacking a dimension of passion that he increasingly felt a need for as the years wore on. Eventually he found that
dimension in the Christianity of his youth, and he returned to that,
even as he continued rigorously with his Zen practice.

And I have known other people, equally rigorous in their
practice, who felt the need after a time to take up some artistic or
intellectual discipline as a supplement to their practice, as another
means of exploring their inmost lives.

I have tried to bring these essential characteristics of the new
spirituality into my own practice and teaching. In order for Zen
Buddhism to be relevant in the next century, our practice must be

existentially, not culturally, based, flexible and tolerant of contradiction, and ecumenical. Some of these features are subtle and have less to do with major changes in the way we do things than with the attitude and understanding we bring to the things we do. But others are not so subtle and they involve some innovative sorts of retreats and programs—many of which I have created in order to fill needs I saw were there.

Our particular lineage of Zen is quite conservative. I appreciate that. Tradition is strong and positive, as far as I am concerned. Doing things that have been done for a long time by respected elders seems more solid to me than making up what works for me today.

And yet a strong aspect of Zen has been to always keep our minds as open as possible, even while our bodies are doing things in the old ways. The founder of our lineage in America, Shunryu Suzuki, coined the phrase *beginner's mind.* "In the expert's mind, there are few possibilities," he wrote. "In the beginner's mind, there are many."

Every morning I get up and go to the meditation hall or zendo. At its center is an altar with a Buddha on it, very much like an altar you would see in a Japanese Zen temple. I wear Japanese robes with outlandishly wide sleeves, a style that was taken into Japanese tradition from the T'ang dynasty in China centuries ago. Our daily chanting service, which is now mostly in English, still has some Japanese and is modeled on the chanting ceremony you would experience in a Japanese Soto Zen monastery. When I lead retreats or monastic practice periods, I conduct the traditional ceremonies and model my talks and statements after those of the teachers of old. I even have a snow-white ceremonial fly whisk that I use for special occasions; it is the same type of whisk used by S'ung dynasty Chinese monks.

I have the sense that in order to really steep ourselves in a tradition, and to receive the benefits of wisdom and depth that it can bring, we must do the daily work of training in a lifestyle that may be restrictive or difficult. Zen may have the reputation of being a "sudden awakening" school of Buddhism, but it doesn't offer any shortcuts.

On the other hand, the attitude with which all of this training and traditional activity is presented can vary quite a bit. Traditionally, it has often been presented as an absolute: *this* is the way to train, *this* is the way to live. And the Zen teacher or master or priest is the authority, a person to be revered and obeyed.

I try to present a much different style. For one thing, I try to emphasize the personal. I try, without being inappropriately friendly or informal, to be as natural and as honest as I can with my students and congregants. I work pretty hard on my practice, but I am certainly not perfect at it, and while I try to understand as much as I can of the wisdom of the past, I have certainly not mastered it. I can—and do—learn from others all the time. I express this to my students, and often tell them stories of my own stupidity or confusion. In fact, "confusion" is a word I often apply to myself, not, I suspect, entirely in its usual sense, but to make the point that I do not have the answers. Each person needs to find answers for him or herself. Although I wear robes in the meditation hall and for formal occasions, and I shave my head, I dress in ordinary Western casual clothing most of the time. I have eschewed all formal titles and am known everywhere by my first name. I appear around the temple not as a revered figure of august proportions but as an ordinary person, and I try to come across that way in all social and work situations: kind, I hope, and considerate with my speech and actions, ordinary and approachable.

This may not sound like anything unusual, but you need to understand the Zen context in order to appreciate it. In days gone by, certainly in Asia, and even here in the West, with Asian as well as Western teachers, there has been quite a cult of the "specialness" of the Zen master. This has been quite counterproductive. If, as I believe, the goal of Zen is to free us so that we are fully able to be ourselves deeply and fully, then focusing attention on the teacher goes against the grain.

So I try to maintain the delicate balance between holding my necessary place as leader and teacher and, at the same time, giving it away completely and letting the student come forward.

In addition to this, I have made a special effort in my lecturing and teaching to always speak inspired by the questions, "What does this have to do with our everyday living? What does this actually mean?"

Religious talk so easily becomes abstract, and despite Zen's reputation for being concrete and illogical, that is no less the case with our tradition. Religious talk, I am convinced, is fundamentally intended as medicine for our human sickness of alienation from self and others. But it can too easily become poison and promote misunderstanding.

We have enough problems already, so it is not necessary to introduce another ideology that we must live up to and with which we can judge each other. Goodness knows there has been plenty of this throughout the history of religions. And we don't need to look to history to see this: Just look at this morning's newspaper or look at your own judgmental and prejudiced mind. So I always take as much care as I can to bring the lofty Zen insight and language down to the everyday.

In the San Francisco Bay area where I live, there is a tremendous amount of Buddhist and ecumenical religious activity. Many religious teachers from all traditions of Buddhism—Vajrayana, Theravada, Zen, Shin, Tibetan, Japanese, Korean, Vietnamese, Chinese, Burmese, Thai—as well as rabbis and ministers and priests and nuns meet with each another and share insights. I find this very valuable, and over the years have given myself permission to be eclectic.

In Soto Zen there is a particular meditation technique that is exclusively used, and this is what I myself practice and mostly teach. But if I encounter a situation or a student for which something else is called for, I do not hesitate to use it. Too much mixing and matching can be counterproductive because steadiness over time is necessary for religious practice to be effective, but I use whatever will work in a particular situation. And I try to be flexible in the same way in my private interviews and other meetings with students. I try to come from a place of listening and discernment, rather than from a stance of preconception about what is acceptable and workable. We all—not just Zen Buddhists—should enhance our practice this way.

An attitude of openness, or at least the effort to be as open as possible (because one never knows whether or not one really is open!) is not, I would say, typical of religion of the past, or, in some places, of the present, but is, as far as I am concerned, a crucial element in our new spirituality.

We Must Refocus on Compassion and Concern for Others

In all religious traditions, compassion and concern for the benefit of others are central. I see this concern as tradition's protective armor: As long as it is kept shining and bright, and at the heart of what is practiced, you can't go wrong. But all too often (and this has sometimes been the case with Zen not only in Asia but here in the West) a tradition loses sight of this, or, if it does not lose sight of it entirely, forgets its centrality. In my teaching I have tried to come back to this point again and again. It is not our insight or our wisdom that counts, I try to tell people. It is our conduct and the warmth of our heart. It is not our brilliance in explaining a text or the physical prowess we display in our upright meditation. It is our kind speech and our beneficial action, our ready smile and our helping hand.

Zen is inherently a very stripped down and austere spirituality, and there is something wonderful in this, especially in our consumer era when we all have so many possessions and interests that we can't keep track of them all. But simplicity need not be standoffish coldheartedness, and it must not be. I harp on this point quite a bit, and, more than harping, I try to demonstrate it in my everyday conduct. We all—not just Zen Buddhists—should enhance our practice this way.

Working with my own mind and heart and with the minds and hearts of people I encounter in my life, I have tried to follow my nose to develop ways of practice that will answer the actual spiritual needs of people. I have not tried to be inventive or innovative. I do not hold that as a value: There is plenty that is new already. I merely do whatever I can to meet conditions that are in front of me.

With that spirit, we have developed at our centers a number of new approaches to Zen practice. We now do nontraditional retreats for business people; we engage very actively in Jewish-Buddhist and Christian-Buddhist dialogue; we engage creatively with the practice, organizing retreats using poetry and other art forms; we take the practice out of the temple, entering prisons, schools, and child care and drug rehab centers to teach meditation; we speak out on social issues; and we emphasize intimate relationship as a form of practice.

In the remainder of this vision for renewed Zen life in America, I want to speak about these areas and how they can transform Zen practice and Zen communities.

New Approaches to Zen Practice: Intimate Relationships

Several years ago I attended a large meditation retreat at the end of which people broke out into various occupational or interest groups for discussion. I decided to attend the business group out of curiosity to see what people in that world would have to say about meditation practice and how it affected their lives.

What I heard surprised and disturbed me a great deal. Person after person spoke of the tremendous stress and grief they felt as they experienced mergers, cutbacks, the pressure for more speed of production, and an increased feeling of a spiraling-out-of-control technology-driven lifestyle, with almost no time for reflection, let alone friendship.

At the end of the discussion I asked whether anyone felt it would be of benefit to have a special retreat for business people, in which these issues could be discussed and explored, with meditation as a backdrop. The response was an overwhelming yes, and so began our ongoing retreat series called Company Time.

Company Time, which I co-lead with several Buddhist students who work in business, has been a very moving experience for me these past few years. We convene several times a year for a weekend during which we practice silent meditation together and take a Buddhist ethical precept and discuss it carefully as it applies specifically to work in the business world. I have been consistently impressed by the numbers of people who feel the need for and, little by little, the possibility of, making work into an occasion for spiritual practice. Company Time has become an ongoing community of support for these people, and many of them come again and again, exchange addresses, and become allies for each other in times between retreats. Many people have used the retreats as occasions to find the courage to change their lives, when that was necessary, or to learn ways of going back into the work place with a renewed vision of what is possible.

The retreats emphasize silent meditation practice very strongly; this practice is absolutely at the heart of what we do. With meditation practice we can have a different kind of conversation: more friendly, less fear-driven, more open-minded. And we can begin to see our conduct, our human problems, in a different light. During the weekend we give people the instruction and encouragement they need to continue to meditate informally in groups or alone at home as a way of opening the heart and finding the silent strength to see what's right and to follow through with it. We encourage them to meditate also in order to find the peace and spaciousness within to sustain what are often difficult and demanding lives.

Our discussions during the course of the retreats are not in the form of the usual corporate offerings that present high concept solutions to perceived problems. Rather, we speak personally and intimately, respecting the immensity of the problems of our time, knowing that no one has answers and that satisfaction will only come through personal integrity and long effort. We emphasize the courage necessary sometimes simply to go on with a good spirit. We hope that the meditation practice, along with some simple Zen teachings, can help people have a wider sense of what is possible. Many of them report that our hope is not unfounded.

Among the techniques we have taught in our retreats is a form of walking meditation that can be used on lunch hour or during a bathroom break; a phone-answering meditation that emphasizes greeting each new caller with freshness; the practice of mantras or affirmations to remind us of our potential freedom in each moment.

Company Time retreats draw an audience of people from a variety of businesses, both for and nonprofit, and there is a great comfort in being able to talk together with people from other companies who may share your problems but not your workplace. Lately I have begun doing similar retreats *in* companies. Brought in by managers or owners who feel that meditation practice will help foster an atmosphere of peacefulness and friendliness among coworkers, I have taught meditation and yoga, and given simple teachings about the application of Buddhist insight to the challenge of business life.

Another series of retreats that I have found to be enormously valuable for others and personally enriching is the series I have been doing with my old friend Rabbi Alan Lew. Called Meditation and Torah, these retreats, the fruit of our long friendship, combine versions of traditional Jewish prayer service with silent meditation practice. They also include times for teaching both Buddhist and Jewish texts, as well as times for sharing and dialogue. We do the retreats in one-day and five-day formats, and they are usually quite emotional and lively, sometimes bringing up much complaining and perplexity, as well as joy and insight.

Alan and I have been dear friends and comrades on the Path for almost thirty years, and we enjoy practicing together and exploring Jewish-Buddhist issues very much. Alan, who became a rabbi after many years of Zen practice, has become a leader in the new Jewish meditation movement, and through him I have been able to learn much about directions in Judaism.

I am quite passionate about the importance of these retreats. The majority of Jews in America are inactive religiously as Jews; it is by far the minority that participate in, or even belong to, congregations. And the congregations themselves seem to be in a time of great transition, feeling a strong need to look for new ways to understand and practice Jewish spirituality. It is beginning to dawn on everyone that European Jewry is quite dormant, Israel can no longer be entirely responsible to hold all of the Jewish heart's need, and in America intermarriage and secularism are having serious effects on the possibility of Jewish survival. Although my practice is as a Zen Buddhist, I have a strong passion for these issues, and I want to help as far as I can. It seems very much as if meditation practice can be an aid and an ally in this time of change for Jewish people.

It seems to me that interreligious dialogue in general is an important practice these days. When our world is so overcome with hatred and deadly misunderstanding of various sorts, it seems clear that all efforts to understand one another in our differences are worthwhile and will build bridges of peace little by little as time goes on. So, in addition to my work with Jewish-Buddhist retreats, I have been very active in recent years with Buddhist-Christian dialogue, taking part in several large events that have brought together leaders from Catholic and Buddhist traditions from all over the world. In 1996 at Thomas Merton's Gethsemani monastery in Kentucky, and again in 1998 in Bodhgaya, India, I participated with His Holiness Dalai Lama and Catholic monastics in significant interreligious meetings that have been enormously illuminating for my own practice. I have made many friends and have opened myself to whole arenas of study that I never knew existed. One of the consequences of this has been my detailed study of the Rule of St. Benedict, the sixth-century monastic rule that still regulates the daily life of Catholic monasteries. These interactions are an example of how Zen Buddhism must strive to be more ecumenical.

Having been a working poet almost all my adult life—scrawling down poems between training periods, publishing books, and doing poetry readings when I could—I have been interested for many years in the relationship between spiritual practice and poetry. Out of this interest I have created a series of retreats that combine the two disciplines.

As with all nontraditional Zen retreats, poetry retreats include meditation practice done in an informal and relaxed setting. This practice is juxtaposed with some writing exercises or reading of poems. For retreats that involve writing, I have created all sorts of techniques for opening up a person's sense of language, so that he or she can make discoveries through writing, rather than simply repeat ideas or emotions that have been floating around in the mind for a long time. These techniques include ways of collaborative writing, timed writing, and the use of found words. The exercises are usually a lot of fun and are presented as experiments rather than as occasions for the creation of Nobel Prize–caliber literature.

Experiments are opening: They do not require evaluation or judgment, only finding out what happens, and so they are generally quite helpful in allowing people free and surprising access to parts of their own deep spirituality that otherwise might never come forth.

Retreats in which we do reading and discussion of poetry are easygoing and sweet. After our meditation practice we meander through a small booklet of poems that I have collected over the years, reading favorites and using the poems as takeoff points for talking about our lives, our spirituality, our joys, and our sorrows. Great poetry has resonance and can provide us quite often with a better mirror for the spirit than traditional religious texts can afford. Poetry brings up the human side, the affective and emotional side, of our religious impulse.

Taking Meditation Practice into the Community

Another important effort I and other Zen teachers have made to transform Zen practice is to take it out of the meditation hall, off of the temple grounds, and into the community in whatever way we can. Starting with the proposition that meditation practice is worthwhile, even transformative, and that it does not depend on a set of religious beliefs and can be used with almost any belief system, or none, we want to share what we have with others wherever they are, especially those who need it most and may not be in a position to find it.

With this thought, our Center in San Francisco has become quite active in offering meditation classes wherever we find a sincere interest in the cultivation of meditation as a tool for the good. We have an extensive prison project that not only offers meditation and yoga classes in local jails and prisons, but also sends books and tapes to prisoners, and offers correspondence. We have done meditation classes in child care centers, drug rehab centers, and churches. I myself have often taught meditation classes in the local schools. We have done classes and special retreats for political activists and teachers, for whom burnout is a constant problem and a spiritual viewpoint probably a necessity for a sustainable active life. These are ways that Zen can "reach out" to the broader world.

The Sacred Practice of Relationships

The final area of practice I want to mention is one I have spent a good deal of effort on over the years—and an area that many Zen teachers are finally focusing on in an effort to fully contextualize our teaching and practice. My efforts in this area have been personal and private, on a one-to-one basis, and yet I feel that this aspect of Zen practice may be the most important, and certainly the most heartwarming, of all. I am speaking of the practice of intimate relationships.

My parents were together for over forty years before my mother's death ended the marriage many years ago. Such a thing was not unusual of course for their generation; in the small community in which I grew up divorce was not completely unknown, but it was rare and it was considered a great failure and a tragedy. In more recent times divorce is so common that my wife and I, who have been married for twenty-three years, feel like very unusual and special people! Marriages that last, in creative and happy ways, are simply not the norm in our time.

There are so many quite funny jokes about the difficulty of relationships, about the impossibility of men and women ever hoping to understand one another, that it is obvious we are all aware of the problem. Men are from Mars, women are from Venus, a popular book tells us, and there are many books that dispense advice about how to do this thing that used to seem so simple: fall in love and stay in love. To be relevant in the future, Zen must address our intimate relationships.

It is clearly not simple, if it ever was. Intimate, long-standing relationships require intelligence, courage, and emotional acumen. Intimate relationship—the need for it and the difficulty of sustaining it—is a powerful element of our new spirituality, whether or not anyone thinks it ought to be. I think that the only way to approach intimate relationship is precisely as a spiritual practice. But how to go about it?

When I am asked this question I often point out that the Buddha, when confronted with the question himself, said, in effect: This one is too hard for me! Since I am sure I cannot handle it, I will start a celibate order of monks and nuns who will strive for spiritual depth without the difficult challenge of married and family life.

If the Buddha thought it was too hard, it's no wonder that it's hard for us!

But it is not impossible. While it is true there isn't much teaching and lore in Zen or Buddhism that speaks directly about marriage, family, or relationships, there is much that is relevant if only we can develop a way of applying and adapting the teachings. This is creative and important work that I have been engaged with for many years, not only in my own personal life, but in the many encounters I have had with students as we have tried to work with this issue in our community over the years.

Our three Zen Centers are not single-sex celibate communities. Both sexes are welcome, and although we have rules against getting involved in inappropriate relationships, we recognize that intimate relationships, if they are conducted lovingly and honorably, can be an important element of a person's spiritual path.

We encourage students to talk frankly with their teachers when they become involved in intimate relationships, and to try to treat the beloved with great kindness and sensitivity, practicing with the relationship as a way of developing one's capacity for compassion and selflessness. Relationships in our community are, as a consequence, never casual, and they are always, or at least almost always, conducted with dignity. I am sometimes frustrated at the amount of time leaders may have to spend working things out when rules are violated or relationships become disentangled, but in the end I feel that it is worthwhile, and there is little I find more moving than two people who have, through spiritual endeavors, found a way to be truly loving toward one another. Such relationships usually inspire and encourage many others on the path and this practice of intimate relationships is necessary to transform Zen Buddhism in the coming years.

Our tradition has a very beautiful marriage ceremony, which involves the couple not only in a commitment to each other, but also to a way of life defined by Zen precepts that gives them the maximum possibility of staying together along the winding path of human change and development. Counseling and encouraging couples and watching them blossom has become an important part of Zen practice.

Our new spirituality may not be so different from the old spirituality in the end. It is really impossible to know how people of the past understood things, how they lived, and how they felt in the intimate texture of the lives they led. Books don't tell us, and no document can ever really show us what things were actually like on the inside long ago. Each generation is different, each individual is unique. Probably all discussions of sameness and difference are really more an exploration of how we feel in the present than about anything in the past, or elsewhere. But I imagine that a spirituality that is not pompous or judgmental, that honors life as life and looks toward happiness and kindness as the essential human birthright, is neither old nor new. It is something that has always been with us, and has always been elusive. Elusive, but not unfindable.

For More Information

"Company Time: A Buddhist
    Meditation Retreat and
    Workshop for People Who
    Work in the Business World"
"Meditation & Torah: Jewish
    Retreats"
Held at:
Green Gulch Farm
1601 Shoreline Highway
Sausalito, CA 94965
Tel: (415) 383-3134
Website: www.sfzc.com

THE PROTESTANT COUNTER REFORMATION

Reverends Lynn and Mark Barger Elliott

Lynn Barger Elliott is an associate pastor at the First Presbyterian Church in Ann Arbor, Michigan:

I graduated from Wheaton College with a degree in philosophy and from Princeton Theological Seminary. My experience as a clergyperson includes being a chaplain at Trenton State Prison and at a New Jersey state psychiatric hospital, preaching in rural churches in Maine, and leading youth programs in Pennsylvania and New Jersey.

Mark Barger Elliott is associate pastor at the First Presbyterian Church in Ann Arbor, Michigan:

I graduated from Cornell University with a degree in English and from Princeton Theological Seminary. Recently, I taught a preaching course at Sacred Heart Seminary and currently I am writing Styles of Preaching, *to be published by Westminister/John Knox Press. I have been a chaplain in St. George's Hospital in London, taught a confirmation class in Germany, preached in small congregations in Brazil, and led youth programs in New York, New Jersey, and Pennsylvania.*

We both care deeply about the future of the Presbyterian church and work to instill in the youth of our church an appreciation of the traditions of our worship service. Our young people, for example, lead two worship services a year, including preaching to a congregation of 800. We currently live in Ann Arbor, Michigan, with our two children, Brendan and Auden.

Sunday mornings aren't what they used to be.

Soccer practice. Roller blading. Project deadlines. Sleeping in. The Sunday paper and a good, hot cup of coffee.

Fewer and fewer members of mainline Protestant churches, it seems, are rustling their children out of bed, straightening their ties in the mirror, and driving to church. Sometime in the past twenty years, Sunday morning went up for grabs and a whole generation of Presbyterians, Methodists, Episcopalians, and Lutherans now consider attending church one option among many for how they will spend it.

And who can blame them? The organ wheezes, the pews are cracked, the carpets are threadbare, and the minister keeps saying, "Please feel free to invite your friends."

On the edge of the twenty-first century, we who work or participate in mainline churches face in many ways the same drastic choice the automobile industry did in the seventies: *We must evolve or face extinction.* We are in dire need of a new vision of what it means to worship God in the new millennium: a vision that crosses denominational lines and appeals to the postmodern need of people to be spiritually nourished as well as entertained.

At each turn in God's history with humanity, we have faced

decisions about how we might worship God. In the Hebrew Scriptures, the patriarchs Abraham and Jacob collected stones and built monuments to mark where they sensed God was present. During the reign of King David, in an era of military skirmishes, the ark of the covenant was housed in a tent and taken from town to town where it would be safe. In an era of peace, David's son, Solomon, built a permanent home for the ark—a magnificent temple where people gathered to worship. When the temple was destroyed by the Babylonians and the Israelites were sent into exile, the religious leaders wondered once again, "What is next?"

In the book of Isaiah, we overhear a conversation between God and the prophet about what the future will hold. For in Babylon, the Israelites would face a smorgasbord of pagan religions that could entice them away from traditional Jewish practices. After hearing Isaiah's concern, God reminds him that God's relationship with the Israelites is constant, though not static. And it will always continue to change. God says, "Do not remember the former things, or consider the things of old. I am about to do a new thing; now it springs forth, do you not perceive it?" (Isaiah 42:9)

On the cusp of the twenty-first century, many of us look around at our friends and neighbors who have left the pews and ask, "What is next?" In our community, for example, sporting events, school meetings, and rehearsals are regularly scheduled on Sunday morning. All this leads to the question: How should we worship God in the twenty-first century? How will we worship when the style and content of our European religious ancestry proves less and less appealing and relevant?

Why Has "The Next Church" Been Dramatically Successful?

Some believe that what is emerging is found in what journalist Charles Trueheart calls "The Next Church."[1] The most prominent of these "Next Churches" is located in an office-style complex in a suburb of Chicago. With an average attendance of over 14,000, Willow Creek has become a model for hundreds of churches all over the world. Its formula intentionally strips the sanctuary of traditional imagery and architecture, and recreates the order of worship to offer something entirely new to the "church shopper."

At Willow Creek you won't find yourself gazing upon a cross at the front of the sanctuary, but upon an artificial pond. At Willow Creek you won't sit in stiff, wooden pews but in cinema-style seating with plush cushions. At Willow Creek you won't be offered a bulletin at the door, but be guided by an "M.C." who guides the congregation between drama, multi-media presentations, musical soloists, and "talks." Worship at Willow Creek is geared toward those who have never set foot in church before and also toward those who drifted away as young adults. Bill Hybels, Willow Creek's minister, writes, "We wanted to be a church for people who thought church was irrelevant but who needed it so desperately."[2]

Of course, not all so-called "Next Churches" have had the phenomenal success of Willow Creek. But in the past fifty years, many nondenominational churches and loosely structured denominations such as the Assemblies of God have opened their doors to an enthusiastic response. For example, our denomination, the mainline Presbyterian Church (USA), has grown 13% between 1964 and 1994 while the Assembly of God denomination has grown 306%.[3]

1. Trueheart, Charles, "The Next Church." *The Atlantic Monthly,* August 1996, p. 52.
2. Hybels, Bill. *Rediscovering Church.* Grand Rapids: HarperCollins, 1995, p. 16.
3. Campolo, Tony, "The Spirit Hasn't Left the Mainline." *Christianity Today,* August 1997, p. 17.

What prompted this significant growth is in many respects *a new reformation.* Pastors such as Bill Hybels have reinterpreted and reformed worship in light of secular culture and taste. Just as Martin Luther reinvented church music in the sixteenth century by transcribing old hymns to bar tunes, so these pastors have bridged the gap between the church and culture by offering congregations bands instead of organs, soloists instead of choirs. Lee Strobel, a former journalist for the *Chicago Tribune,* writes about the first time he attended Willow Creek: "The songs were a kind of driving soft-rock, and I thought they were great in spite of the Christian lyrics." One of the reasons these "Next Churches" are appealing is that the transition from Sunday morning at home to Sunday morning at church is not that difficult or jarring.

We Need a New Protestant Counter Reformation

So where does this leave those of us who worship in mainline denominations? In many ways, it leaves us with a dire call to action. Just as the Catholic church responded to Calvin and Luther with a Counter Reformation, drawing upon the best of their tradition and yet responding to the innovations of the Reformation, so must Protestant churches respond to these "Next Churches" and organize our own "Protestant Counter Reformation." The time has come to gather our most creative people—worship leaders, lyricists, architects, and composers—and craft a new way to worship God. A style is needed that will build upon the foundation of our traditions as well as respond to and incorporate changing cultural tastes and needs.

Of course, just as the reforms of Luther and Calvin prompted revolts and imprisonment for their followers, so too will any new reformation be met with suspicion and anxiety. The stakes are high. Disagreements over which hymns to discard, which ones to add, are to be expected. Church leaders should expect to spend hours pulling out their hair about whether to continue to use the old hymnal or to project words on an overhead screen. Those opposed to change will no doubt write letters and petitions to keep the organ from being mothballed or used with guitars and drums.

But ultimately, do we have any choice? Charles Trueheart, a life-long Episcopalian who spent an entire year visiting contemporary churches while researching an article on them for an *Atlantic Monthly* article, concluded, "I look to few things as warmly as singing great lungfulls of old hymns and kneeling . . . at the communion rail . . . I also wonder . . . whether my church is not in danger of wither-ing away. And whether it doesn't deserve that fate if it doesn't get intentional, and soon."[4] Just as Luther and Calvin rose to the task of reinterpreting the structure and content of worship for the sixteenth century, now it falls upon us to "reform" the way we worship, focus-ing ourselves first of all on the words and music of faith.

Worship Is a Verb and Must Foster a Response

Every summer in Taize, a small town in France, over 100,000 young people come from all over Europe to a small monastic com-munity set among the rolling hills of the French countryside. The order is led by Brother Roger, a man who after World War II estab-lished a sanctuary where Christians from all denominations might worship, commit themselves to Christ, and be trained to serve the poor.

4. Trueheart, p. 58.

To create such a place, Brother Roger began by carefully shaping the worship of the community, in particular the style of music the community would sing. One of his brothers, Jacques Berthier, wrote simple choruses that could be sung in a chantlike manner and in different languages. For example, if you were to attend a Taize service you would find no hymnal. When you sing at Taize, the Holy Spirit leads. You might sing a chorus for five, ten, fifteen minutes, or until the congregation decides to move on to another song. This open-ended style enables everyone to learn the tune and to participate. Taize's music has been well received by Protestants and Catholics alike. In fact, we incorporate their chants into our weekly worship and our Ash Wednesday service.

In 1993, we traveled to Taize to see for ourselves why this music has become so popular. What we found was a simple sanctuary and a congregation that sang with its eyes closed, their hands outstretched, and their bodies prostrated. Many spoke of it as a sacred experience. The lesson we took from Taize was how crucial it is for church music to foster an emotional and spiritual response in a congregation—for toes to start tapping, hands to clap, eyes to close.

Robert Webber helpfully suggests that a way to foster such music is to understand that "Worship is a *verb*. It is not something that is done to us or for us, but by us."[5] For example, what made Calvin and Luther successful was their desire to return worship to the people, especially with congregational singing. In the previous several hundred years, only ministers and choirs could sing in worship. Calvin took a different approach and encouraged Psalms to be

5. Webber, Robert E. *Worship Is a Verb.* (Dallas: Word Publishing, 1984), p. 12.

sung with no professional or choral leadership.[6] In other words, the focus was no longer on the ministers who stood apart from the congregation. Everyone sang, read scripture in their own language, and prayed. Soren Kierkegaard, the Danish philosopher, built on the work of the reformers by suggesting that what really occurs during worship is that the congregation is on stage—and God is the audience. The minister, the choir, are all really offstage, whispering stage directions. That is our future.

Worship must continually return to the people. The community of Taize, for example, does not offer majestic choirs or chamber orchestras, but simple, elegant music that invites each soul to respond. Those who attend Taize services are not observers *but participants*. The worship service creates a space for them to be themselves: to dance, to sit in the aisles with their legs crossed, to sway to the music. Emotions are welcomed: joy, sadness, contrition, however and wherever the Holy Spirit leads.

Recently, we observed what can happen when worship becomes a *verb*. The congregation we serve is on the University of Michigan campus. Our congregation truly appreciates the classical repertoire of Bach, Brahms, and Beethoven. But this past Easter, the University of Michigan gospel choir came to our church for a special concert. For fifteen minutes, our congregation sang gospel songs and clapped, stood, and sang as loud as it could. While some grumbled about the volume, most breathlessly whispered, "That was wonderful." Their hands might have been sore from clapping, their throats raw, but they had joyfully offered something to God and that made all the difference. Frederick Buechner writes that this is exactly what should happen every Sunday:

6. Sanders, Shelly. *The Register.* Office of Theology and Worship, Presbyterian Church, Summer 1998, p. 31.

To worship means . . . to sing songs for Him . . . in general rejoice in Him and make a fool of yourself for Him the way lovers have always made fools of themselves for the one they love. A Quaker Meeting, a Pontifical High Mass, the Family Service at First Presbyterian, a Holy Roller Happening—unless there is an element of joy and fool- ishness in the proceedings, the time would be better spent doing something useful.[7]

In Taize, and on that Sunday at First Presbyterian, we respond- ed with our hands and with our hearts. God said to Isaiah, "I am about to do a new thing." Could that new thing be a transformation in the way we sing in worship? Might that mean congregations that sing Brahms occasionally sing a chant or a gospel song?

Unfortunately, our churches often view music outside of the traditional church canon with suspicion, and at times with derision. But this reliance on classical music has often forced choir directors to hire professional singers to keep everyone on pitch. We strive for the very best in church music, but sometimes reduce a joyful noise to a carefully constructed performance. A older woman recently told us she was leaving our church because she didn't like sitting through all that "performance music."

Some of our fascination with perfection arises from the fear of making a mistake and displeasing God. In Denver, Colorado, for example, a downtown Presbyterian church holds a dress rehearsal every Saturday to make sure all is perfect: from the anthems to the sermon. This thirst to give to God our best effort is admirable, but perhaps it would be better to let the Spirit of God take hold—and, as Buechner suggests, look a little foolish.

7. Buechner, Frederick. *Wishful Thinking: A Seeker's ABC.* San Francisco: HarperSanFrancisco, 1993, p. 122.

There are, of course, different ways to reach and to appeal to people through music. A glance back through the Bible reveals a variety of worship styles: Miriam, the sister of Moses, grabbed a tambourine and led the women in singing and dancing to celebrate God's guiding them through the Red Sea; the Levitical priests followed strict rules in their ritual sacrifices; the psalmists wrote of singing and using music to express joy as well as disappointment and anger before God.

Biblical history reminds us there is no one way to worship God. The new things that are springing forth might be electric guitars and drums or they could be a return to ancient forms of worship.

In downtown Seattle, for example, an Episcopal church often starts its evening service with ancient Gregorian chants and silence. The entire sanctuary is lit with candles. At times the church is so full that people sit along the walls. One participant said, "It doesn't matter who you are or why you are here. You can be quiet and peaceful together."[8] Why do the students come? Perhaps because the music is so unlike what they listen to in their dorms. It offers soothing rhythms and cadences. It whispers of another time and place.

Churches such as this one remind us we need not toss out our musical heritage, but thoughtfully and prayerfully evaluate and expand our repertoire. The Catholic Church did not adopt everything Luther and Calvin offered but chose what was fit and appropriate. We believe what is called for is a time of *discernment*. There are times when we should sing in church the way we sing when we wake up or commute to work. We should develop surveys to determine what music makes our pulses quicken—a rock anthem, a simple chorus, a Gregorian chant, a Bach cantata? General William

8. "The Faithful Are Casual At This Sunday Service." *New York Times*, March 16, 1997, p. 14.

Booth of the Salvation Army reportedly said, "Why does the devil get all the good tunes?" It is time to find those tunes and to bring them back to church.

Much is at stake. We need both conservators and innovators—those who push the envelope and those who drag their heels, for this period of discernment will be difficult.

Our staff of eight at First Presbyterian, for example, is deeply divided about what that repertoire might include. Some of us say, "Classical music is dead. No one buys it or likes it except for a very small minority. We should have more contemporary music, guitars, drums, synthesizers." Others say, "But what about quality, or preserving a tradition? For years people have listened to this music. I grew up with hymns and I don't like choruses." Of course, both groups are right. We both agree that what will draw people back to church is not organs or guitars, Bach or the Beatles, but whether or not our music lets others worship God with their heart, soul, and mind. People will return to churches when we sing music that touches them emotionally and spiritually, and compels them to again deepen their relationship with God.

God said to Isaiah and God says to us, "I am about to do a new thing." On All Saint's Day that might mean Brahms' Requiem; on a dreary Sunday in February it might mean a foot-stomping gospel song; on the Fourth of July it might mean a rock 'n' roll anthem led by the youth group. Above all, we must choose the very best of what is new and blend it with the very best of the old and the familiar. Some of that work, for example, is already occurring in the Presbyterian Church (USA), which will soon publish a supplemental hymnal with contemporary hymns.

Every year, a lobster sheds its skin in a process called "molting." During a brief period of time, it sits vulnerable on the ocean floor without protection as it grows a new shell. Now is the time for us to shed our old protective shells, and to sit vulnerable on the ocean floor. If we do that, then perhaps God will work inside us to create a new thing. Five hundred years ago, the Catholic Church listened to Calvin and Luther, debated, and then forged new ways to worship. The time has come for us to follow in the footsteps of our Catholic brothers and sisters.

Dusting Off the Frescos: We Need to Revitalize Our Words

The second area that deserves attention is the liturgy: the words we say in worship. Mainline Protestant churches love words! We have elaborate prayers, written responses, and, at times, lengthy sermons. In our tradition we use a bulletin to describe the order of service and the words one is expected to say during worship. These words can be meaningful and helpful, but congregations might now be experiencing "word overload." Lyle E. Schaller writes, "The generation born after 1968 has been heavily influenced by television in general and MTV in particular . . . A critical implication is to place less emphasis on the spoken and printed word."[9]

Neil Postman adds,

> Think of Richard Nixon or Jimmy Carter or Billy Graham, or even Albert Einstein, and what will come to your mind is an image, a picture of a face, most likely a face on a television screen. Of words, almost nothing will come to mind. This is the difference between thinking in a word-centered culture and thinking in an image-centered culture.[10]

9. Lyle E. Schaller as quoted in *New Results,* June 1995, p. 14.
10. Postman, Neil. *Amusing Ourselves to Death.* New York: Penguin Books, 1985, p. 61.

Many of the "Next Churches" have already responded to this shift and replaced read responses and sermons with drama, overhead screens, and film clips to communicate their message.

Postman, however, warns that one of the hazards of moving from a word-based culture to an image-based culture is that we will cease to exchange ideas with one another. It is more difficult for images to communicate nuanced ideas or concepts than words. In fact, one of the critiques of the "Next Churches" is they have made worship *too comfortable*. In a move away from words, in particular old, time-worn words such as "sin" and "confession," they have gutted worship of its historical integrity and purpose.

By appealing primarily to our emotions, they have lost the ability to communicate difficult or complicated concepts. As Marva Dawn writes in *Reaching Out without Dumbing Down*, "In a society doing all it can to make people cozy, somehow we must convey the truth that God's Word, rightly read and heard, will shake us up. It will kill us, for God cannot bear our sin and wants to put to death our self-centeredness."[11]

Our words and ideas hold us together. And that familiarity, we must remember, can be as tempting a reason to return to church as a view of the crystal clear lake. When Dan Wakefield, a novelist, returned to church in his middle years, he wrote:

> I had simply assumed I did not know people who went to church, yet here they were, with intellects intact, worshiping God. Once inside the church myself, I understood the appeal. No doubt my friends and neighbors found, as I did, relief and refreshment in connecting with age-old

11. Dawn, Marva J. *Reaching Out without Dumbing Down*. Grand Rapids: Eerdmans, 1995, pp. 205–206.

rituals, reciting psalms and singing hymns . . . There was
a calm reassurance in the stately language of litanies and
chants . . . I was grateful for the sense of shared
reverence.[12]

And yet, despite experiences such as Wakefield's, we must
transform the words of worship in order to be relevant to people in
the future. Many successful "Next Churches" have consulted with
what in professional circles are called liturgical architects who, after
taking a hard look at their beams and bearing walls, determined
they must go. In those churches, no one misses a read response or a
confession of sin. However, while some of our churches might consider adding a contemporary hymn or two, few would willingly discard the entire form and structure of their worship service.

Which leaves us in an awkward place. Fewer and fewer of us
feel inspired while reading aloud in worship, or listening to a minister talk for twenty minutes, or hearing the word "sin" in worship. Yet
that is how and what we communicate with one another.
Furthermore, every year communities that surround our churches
buy fewer and fewer books and watch more and more T V How can
we reasonably expect them to pay attention to our written prayers,
to our sermons, to our words?

What we believe is needed is a judicious renovation of the
words we use in worship. Not a full-scale demolition, as the "Next
Churches" have undertaken. But a recognition that blueprints must
be pulled out and a determination made about which walls must go
and which are worth restoring.

Harvard Divinity School's Dean Sperry tells a story about a
Dutch Reformed Church in Holland that worships in an old Roman

12. Wakefield, Dan. *Returning: A Spiritual Journey.* New York: Penguin, 1988, p. 15.

Catholic church. As members of the congregation exit the church, says Sperry, they bow to a bare white wall at the back of the church. They do this out of tradition, each generation passing it on to the next. One day, however, workmen discovered underneath this blank wall a beautiful fresco of the Virgin Mary. A century before, reformers had painted over it in their iconoclastic zeal against the veneration of images. A hundred years later, no one had ever seen the painting, no one knew it was even there. But it was tradition to bow, so everybody bowed.[13]

Underneath and supporting the worship services of our churches are beautiful frescos covered with dust and obscured from view. We have forgotten they exist and, in many respects, we have forgotten why we might bow on our way out of church. If we are to reform and renew our liturgy we believe that there are three frescos we must restore and recover: The first is a sense of awe, the second a sense of restraint, and the third a sense of the human condition.

A Sense of Awe

Recently we read through the entire Bible. It took us a year, Genesis to Revelation. No shortcuts. As we closed the last chapter we realized one theme surfaced again and again—never take God for granted! Scripture continually teaches us to consider God as Creator, Lord, as One too awesome to lay eyes upon. In our desire to make worship more comfortable, more user-friendly, we have sometimes claimed a familiarity with God that no Biblical figure would assume. No prophet or King in the Bible would approach God as casually as we do. Annie Dillard once asked:

---

13. As quoted in a sermon by Michael Lindvall on August 31, 1997, in First Presbyterian Church, Ann Arbor, Michigan.

Why do people in churches seem like cheerful, brainless tourists on a packaged tour of the Absolute? . . . On the whole, I do not find Christians, outside of the catacombs, sufficiently sensible of conditions. Does anyone have the foggiest idea what sort of power we so blithely invoke? . . . It is madness to wear ladies' hats and velvet hats in church; we should all be wearing crash helmets. Ushers should issue life preservers and signal flares; they should lash us to our pews.[14]

In the temple in Jerusalem was a room that contained the "Holy of Holies." Once a year, on the Day of Atonement, only one person, the High Priest, could enter to atone for the sins of Israel. The room was considered too holy for anyone else to enter. Two gold cherubim spread their wings above the Holy of Holies, facing each other. When the priest entered, according to tradition, he had to approach the Holy of Holies and say the name of God, a name made up of four letters of the Hebrew alphabet, a name no one quite knew how to pronounce. In case he said it wrong, or was impure in some way, a rope was tied around his leg so that he might be dragged out.

Haven't we lost that sense of awe and reverence? While making worship user-friendly with plush seats and overhead projectors, haven't we forgotten to tie a rope around our legs lest we mispronounce God's name? What would happen if we reminded ourselves that it is a fearful thing to come into the presence of God? What if we believed that worship demands our utmost attention and our best effort since everything, including our very lives, is at stake? What would happen to our worship services, and to us, if we

14. Dillard, Annie. *Teaching a Stone to Talk*. New York: Harper & Row, 1982, p. 40.

approached worship with a lump in our throat and a wary eye toward the cross? Would ministers make pointless jokes from the pulpit and choirs go through the motions? Would our attention drift?[15] If we really knew what kind of God we were worshiping, wouldn't we fall on our knees in the realization that nothing else is as important or as crucial than to worship God? This is a fresco waiting to be rediscovered.

A Sense of Restraint

In her book *When God Is Silent,* Barbara Brown Taylor observes that one of the ways to revitalize our worship, to dust off our "soiled, tired language," is to restrain ourselves when we talk about God. In other words, too often we let ourselves ramble, muck about for any old idea, instead of being still, and silent. This idea came to her after receiving a letter from a friend who wrote,

> I think a vast majority of people are sitting in the pews with parched lips. They are so thirsty that they have lost their ability to listen, to speak, or to think. But one big gulp of Gatorade is not the answer. They will drown. Their thirst is so great that it requires a series of sips much like parched fields require a series of gentle rains.[16]

Taylor writes that to approach worship and preaching with restraint does not mean "withholding God's word," but rather "reaching for more reverence in the act of publicly speaking about God." And of course, such reverence toward speaking of God winds its way throughout our church history, in particular in the monastic tradition.

To help dust off this fresco, Taylor offers the image of the

15. Lindvall, Michael, from an article to be published in *Interpretation* on Revelation 4:1–11.
16. Brown Taylor, Barbara. *When God Is Silent.* Boston: Cowley, 1998, pp. 85–86.

church as an ark. An ark where, in the words of Max Pickard, we gather to save ourselves from the "flood of noise outside."[17] Inside this ark, we are offered silence, sanctuary, a place to rest. Inside, we speak with hushed tones and offer only our best words, the few words that as Taylor writes, "we have dug up with our own hands . . . [and] brought back with our own encounter with the silence . . . in a word-clogged world the only words that stand a chance of getting people's attention are simple, honest words that come from everyday life."[18] Taylor challenges those who speak words in worship to make the extra effort to listen, to pay attention, and to discover the word God is speaking to them and then communicate only that, in whatever measure it comes.

A Sense of the Human Condition

A final fresco to uncover and restore is our historical commitment to address the entire spectrum of the human condition: the joys and sorrows, successes and failures of being a human being. One of the sacred parts of our worship is a recognition that we need time every week to come before God with our sins and transgressions. All of us are, at various times, sinner and saint. Sometimes we count our blessings on two hands, but at other times we proceed silently, quietly, praying for a second chance. Craig Barnes writes:

> When we confess our sins in worship, I can't help but look out over the congregation. I see men and women who, like me, are knocking themselves out to get life right. Tragically, that is the cause of much of the sin we are confessing. "O Lord, I have sinned against you and am in need of your mercy." These are the truest words I have said all

17. Ibid, pp. 96–98.
18. Ibid, pp. 100–101.

week. Now I am ready, frightened but ready, to hear what God has to say.[19]

This fresco was etched by the writers of the Bible, writers like David who spoke of our need to confess our sins and have them washed clean like snow. In the following years, people such as Luther and Calvin helped craft our liturgy into what we might call a dance, with four distinct steps. The first step enters the sanctuary and recognizes the presence of God; the second reflects on that presence of God; the third, in response to that holy presence, remembers areas of our lives where we have fallen short of God's example and through confession seeks forgiveness. The final step turns to the Word of God to receive nourishment and to go into the world empowered as children of God.

Many of the "Next Churches" have taught themselves a new dance. They leave out a step or two, rearrange the order, and believe that our steps have gone out of fashion. But their dance is not our dance. If we were to remove the step of confession, we would stumble, lose our rhythm, and fall on our faces. And we have nothing to be ashamed of. The dance we call our worship speaks eloquently about what it means to be human. All we need to do is remind people these are not ancient rituals we perform for the sake of tradition, but rituals we do for the care of our souls.

19. Barnes, Craig, "Taking Liturgy Seriously . . . Sort Of." ReNEWS, February 1993, p. 11.

We Must Be Places Where the Deepest Questions and Needs Are Met

As Karl Barth commented when plans were being made to renovate Penn Station in New York, "Tearing down the old station is not difficult, nor is building the new one. What is difficult is tearing down the old station and building the new one while keeping the trains running on time."

The challenge before the mainline Protestant church is to do just that: tear down the old while building a new and keeping the trains running. This new renovation, or reformation, demands creativity, patience, and passion from our pastors, church musicians, and members. But in the spirit of Calvin and Luther, the time has come to once again proclaim the gospel in ways people can understand and hear. If we fail, then we will undoubtedly have, in the words of Charles Trueheart, "more pew than flock, more history than future."

If we do not, those passing by will soon consider us as mere curators of old cathedrals and quaint rituals, and not what we are—communities where their deepest questions and needs might be met.

CREATING AN ORTHODOX JUDAISM THAT MATTERS

Rabbi Yosef Kanefsky

I am an Orthodox rabbi. Contrary to what everyone seems to assume about

Orthodox rabbis, I did not grow up in a rabbinic family. I did, however,

have the great fortune of growing up in a home and in a community in

which Orthodoxy was the life and

breath of existence. My parents'

home was always kosher, Saturday

was always Shabbat, my father and

my siblings and I attended our

Orthodox synagogue every week

(Mom is now a regular, too), and my parents sacrificed to ensure that we

would all attend Orthodox schools for at least twelve years.

By the middle of high school, even though I was enjoying my studies,

I began to sense that something was wrong somewhere. Religious instruc-

tion was flecked with a disdain for things not Jewish, for Jews not

Orthodox—and for Jews not as Orthodox as we felt we were. There was

subtle (and sometimes not so subtle) bigotry and intolerance that was

somehow thought not to be contrary to our religious beliefs. And there was
an insensitivity to the desire of Orthodox women who desired greater
opportunities for religious expression. It became clear to me that there were
serious flaws in the system.

After Yeshiva University, I entered rabbinical school and began a
master's program in medieval Jewish history. I had no intention of entering
the rabbinate. Too many congregational rabbis seemed frustrated and
burned out. The staid, traditional synagogue didn't seem like the place
where crusty preconceptions could be challenged, or where fresh, even con-
troversial, ideas could be broached. Instead, I planned to be a teacher.

Accidentally, two years after graduation, I found myself as an assis-
tant rabbi at the Hebrew Institute of Riverdale.

It was there, under the tutelage of Rabbi Avi Weiss, that I understood
the synagogue's potential to be a place of creative experimentation and
bold revolutions. I've now been the rabbi at B'nai David-Judea
Congregation in Los Angeles for three years. It, too, is populated by
Orthodox Jews whose love for the tradition requires them to also
see what's wrong with the tradition, and to work hard toward making
it right.

And so, I am an Orthodox rabbi because I believe in Orthodox
Judaism's potential to mold a community that embodies the highest

religious ideals and that lives a religiously and ethically holy life. My vision for Orthodox Judaism that follows is designed to be constructive. Even my parents, to whom I have sent a copy, know that.

Orthodoxy of any sort is a tough game. In an orthodox system, tradition isn't just *an* argument, it usually is *the* argument. And there is no more powerful evidence of the correctness of a given practice or belief than its durability over generations. A religiously motivated vision for change, for adaptation, for departure from ingrained norms, is virtually by definition out of place. This has proven to be particularly true in the case of late twentieth-century Orthodox Judaism. And this is what has made the journey that like-minded colleagues and I have begun toward creating a new, more open, more world-engaging vision for Orthodoxy—in short, for an Orthodoxy that really matters—particularly challenging. Underlying our effort is the rejection of the premise that the words "Orthodox" and "new" cannot appear in the same sentence. To the contrary, we believe that the two great questions that Orthodoxy seeks to answer are: "What is the proper way to live?" and "What is the proper way to change?"

Of course, a few words of explanation are in order about why we even think that Orthodoxy needs this new vision. After all, the argument could well be made that Orthodoxy is thriving. Left for dead after the Holocaust, the movement has proved that predictions of its demise were not only premature, but absolutely wrong. Orthodox day schools and synagogues grow and multiply, Orthodox families tend to be larger than the average American

Jewish family, and the Orthodox community exudes a palpable, well-earned sense of self-confidence (even an unfortunate touch of triumphalism) as it heads into the next century. The "new vision" of which we speak might even be considered something of a betrayal by those who are responsible for Orthodoxy's revival—that small number of souls who courageously decided to hold on to the old ways, come what may and at whatever price.

The reason we now press for a new vision is that we believe the era of religious freedom we currently enjoy demands that we renew our commitment to being the "kingdom of priests" God asked us to be. For centuries, our strength and our outward vision were sapped by constantly worrying about physical and spiritual survival. But now, at a point in history in which, thank God, we don't need to be preoccupied with sheer survival, we are absolutely obliged to emerge from our defensive, preservationist crouch, and again become the kind of world-transforming force that God intended us to be. It is a time for renewal, and renewal demands that we look at ourselves carefully and take seriously the notion that Judaism is one of the great religions of the world.

Another challenge could be raised against our "new vision." Don't more world-engaging, more open models of Judaism already exist? Is this not the thrust of Reform Judaism? Might not Judaism's Conservative movement be a more logical address for our Nuevo-Orthodox vision? Why don't my colleagues and I just move elsewhere?

We stay inside Orthodoxy for two reasons. One is that we are committed to the Orthodox belief system, and to its methods of legal interpretation. Second, we believe, as I alluded above, that Orthodoxy has a unique potential for religious greatness, a unique potential for growing a truly great Jewish community.

We Have a Unique Potential—and a Unique Problem: Finding the Correct Balance Between Tradition and Change

I'll invoke one of my favorite rabbinic anecdotes to illustrate where Orthodoxy's special power and potential comes from. Several summers ago, on a Friday afternoon, I received a phone call from a congregant who was vacationing with his family at a beach house in the Hamptons at the eastern end of New York's Long Island. He had a straightforward, technical question for me: How *early* in the day could he and his family accept the Sabbath. I was deeply moved by the question. It captured the complete commitment to and deep love for tradition that characterizes the Orthodox community. The desire to fulfill God's word is so thoroughly woven into the soul that the accepting of the Sabbath is not perceived as accepting restrictions and limitations upon our activities, but as the opportunity to enter into holy space.

Jews who are committed to the Orthodox tradition do not make a cost/benefit analysis when it comes to the sacrifices of time, energy, and money that are inevitably a part of living by the demands of Jewish law and of educating their children to do the same. The commitment is absolute, and the results speak for themselves. Orthodox parents are wonderfully successful at raising children who remain true to Orthodoxy. Our community has great passion and deep faith, and our children imbibe this. The power of the Orthodox community to be a religious force for positive social and religious change would appear to be immense.

The challenge is to get the Orthodox community to recognize what it is capable of achieving if it only grasped the larger picture. The reason that this is not a simple challenge is that the commitment to tradition that invests us with our unique energy is the very factor that renders us spiritually irrelevant in many ways. Our attachment to the past and our resistance to (and suspicion of) change clearly functions as a double-edged sword.

There exists a wide and well-founded perception that Orthodox Jews don't live in or meaningfully engage the contemporary world. Even so-called "modern Orthodox" Jews who often have post-graduate degrees and hold positions in the most rarified strata of the professional world, often live bifurcated lives. When the workday is done, we return to our religious and intellectual Orthodox ghetto where we neatly divide the world into "Jews" and "non-Jews," and classify all knowledge and ideas and values as either "Torah-based" or "secular." Torah-based is considered relevant to religious life, and appropriate for our religious energies; anything that is secular is just the opposite. As a result, we tend to not grapple with or engage *in religious terms* the phenomena and events that lie outside our highly circumscribed arena of religious relevance.

One of the most appalling expressions of this tendency appeared in a recently published memoir that Rabbi Moshe Meiselman wrote about his uncle, the late Rabbi Joseph Soloveitchik—a figure of giant scholarship and leadership who is regarded as having been the intellectual and spiritual father of twentieth-century modern Orthodoxy.[1] Concerned that Soloveitchik is often portrayed as having had broad interests and that he brought his religious vision to bear on issues outside the immediate Orthodox world, Meiselman writes, "Some people have portrayed [my uncle] as the universal man, deeply concerned with the universal moral

---

1. "The Rav, Feminism and Public Policy." *Tradition*, 1998, vol. 33, no. 1, p. 27.

and social issues of the day . . . This is absurd . . . in all of [his] concerns he was extremely parochial." It is horrifying and frightening that Meiselman believes that he is flattering his uncle with these words. Whether they are an accurate representation or not, they keenly reflect Orthodoxy's "relevance" problem. The problem becomes all the more acute, of course, as we move rightward along the Orthodox spectrum, where higher education is eschewed altogether and social contact with non-Jews virtually doesn't exist.

There are two primary reasons for this isolationist worldview. The first is historical. Centuries of physical and spiritual persecution have ingrained the message that the people of the world and their ideas threaten the integrity and even the survival of our people and our ideas. Thus, withdrawing from the outside has become a retreat into safety. And even today, in an era free of overt religious oppression, many Orthodox Jews (along with other Jews and people of other faiths) still feel besieged by the values and ideals of the "outside." It is understandable that they would regard contemporary attitudes toward sexuality, materialism, and moral relativism as threats to traditional religious values. As a result, the reflex of intellectual, social, and religious wall-building persists.

But this historical explanation can only account for so much. It cannot explain, for example, the near total absence of Orthodox involvement in general social action, or our refusal to engage in any kind of serious theological dialogue with non-Orthodox Judaism (the vast majority of the religious Jewish community). It cannot explain why we tend to battle rather than engage the most promising developments within our society (for example, the advancement of the position of women in the intellectual and political realms). It cannot explain why, to most of the world, Orthodox Judaism does not matter.

Ultimately, the explanation for all of this is rooted in the same absolute commitment to tradition that is our strength. Because of that commitment, we have been unable to distinguish between changing religious *law* (which Orthodoxy approaches with the greatest caution), and changing our understanding of and attitudes toward the ultimate *objectives* of our law. It doesn't come naturally to us to think in new and different terms, to ask, "How does my observance affect not only me and my family, but also the world at large?"

This problem is compounded by the fact that a community deeply committed to tradition tends not to possess a mechanism for religiously examining ideas that arise outside the tradition. And the truth, of course, is that if we *were* to conduct such evaluations, we would realize that non-Jewish western society has generated many important ethical ideals, such as tolerance, democracy, equal rights. We would recognize that modern scholarship has much to add to our understanding of scripture and of Jewish history, and we should also be thinking about the religious and intellectual issues that non-Orthodox Jewish movements have been grappling with.

All of these would require changes in our traditional thought and attitudes—changes laden with exciting potential. Our general reluctance to make these changes has hampered our effectiveness and diminished our relevance as a religious community. Non-Orthodox Jews rightly ask, "Of what ultimate value is a religious community that speaks only to itself? Of what relevance is a religious community that does not engage with the political and intellectual events of the day, and that has nothing to say to the world outside itself? What's the point of being part of a religious community that ultimately does not matter?" These are critical questions. This is where the new vision for Orthodoxy must begin to build.

The familiar response from conservative Orthodox colleagues that even the slightest change in our religious philosophy places us atop a slippery slope that could ultimately lead to our dissolution should not be dismissed casually. But the recognition that irrelevance will also lead us to dissolution must likewise be understood. We need to find the correct balance between tradition and change if we are to escape a fate of chronically unfulfilled potential. We must think about the things that we do, and what we hope to achieve through doing them. Let's look at Sabbath observance as a model for what we can envision ritual devotion to be.

Observing the Sabbath on Tuesday

It's all well and good to begin your Sabbath in the Hamptons as early on Friday afternoon as possible. It's all well and good to regard Sabbath observance as the epitome of Jewish observance. But if a Jew observes the Sabbath and nobody sees the results, has the Jew observed the Sabbath? The same question can be asked regarding the performance of any *mitzvah* (a commanded holy act). Our return journey to relevance begins with changing the traditional way in which we understand and think about the goals of Jewish ritual life. We must re-understand what it really means to have fulfilled a *mitzvah*. The criterion for "fulfillment" that we need employ is drawn from the work of a late thirteenth-century scholar, the anonymous author of the *Sefer HaChinuch* (The Book of Instruction). He wrote that the reason we perform *mitzvot* is that "the heart is drawn after the deeds."[2] The performance is intended to constantly shape and reshape our entire system of personal con-

2. *The Book of Instruction*, Mitzvah #20.

duct. By this measure, I would argue that a Jew has not truly observed the Sabbath unless the world sees the results on Tuesday.

How can observance of Sabbath express itself on Tuesday? Let's begin by asking a more fundamental question: What is the underlying premise of Sabbath observance? We work for six days and rest on the seventh because God worked for six days and rested on the seventh after creating the world. And what does our replication of the Divine work schedule suggest to us? It should suggest that on the six days of the week that we work, we perceive ourselves as employees in the Divine workshop who have been charged with maintaining and enhancing our heavenly employer's project. And what is the message of refraining from writing on the Sabbath? It is to understand that when we *do* write—on the other six days—we do so according to God's exacting specifications. We write only the truth, and do not obfuscate. We write only well of others, giving them the benefit of the doubt whenever possible.

Our writing needs to be free of offensive language and insensitive references. We write on God's letterhead. This is what it ultimately means to observe the Sabbath.

And what is the message of not having others do work for us on the Sabbath? It is that when we *do* have others working for us, we value them as God values them. Our workplaces must be suffused with respect, fairness, and honesty. This is how Sabbath observance and Sabbath observers come to *matter*. Similar discussions can be had concerning refraining from commercial activity on the Sabbath, and refraining from killing even insects, or plucking leaves on the seventh day. It's really all about how we *do* conduct commerce, and how we *do* interact with God's natural environment on Tuesday, Thursday, and Sunday.

This past year, our synagogue became the first in the country to work on a Habitat for Humanity site on a Sunday, rather than on Habitat's usual Saturday workday. Of course, this opportunity to help house those who need homes is inherently and incredibly worthwhile. But next year, I will couple our Habitat workday with a seminar on the previous Saturday, on the laws of not building on the Sabbath. The message will simply be that we observe the Sabbath fully and totally when we don't build on Saturday, and then build on Sunday.

A similar approach can also be applied to each of the major areas of Orthodox ritual practices. Take prayer, for example. For prayer to matter and to be relevant, prayer's impact must extend far beyond the moment of prayer itself. If we train our hearts to follow our deeds, we will understand that one of the reasons we pray three times daily and recite blessings throughout the day is that it compels us to be constantly ready to stand in the Divine presence.

Once, at a reunion of my wife's family, I overheard a woman telling about when her newly Orthodox nephew came to visit overnight. "He was constantly praying," she said, her voice reflecting simple amazement more than anything else. "He got up in the morning and prayed. When he washed his hands, he prayed. When he went to the bathroom, he prayed. He prayed before he ate, and after he ate. He prayed in the afternoon, in the evening, and one more time before he went to sleep. He prayed, and prayed, and prayed."

I was laughing to myself, because as strange as it sounds, that's exactly what we do. There is a prayer or a blessing for virtually any occurrence. But what a powerful spiritual engine this is! The knowledge that at any given time we are only hours away, or perhaps minutes away, from our next prayer demands that we be in a constant state of worthiness for addressing God. We need to be worthy, at every minute, in the eyes of the One who "opens His hand and feeds every living being,"[3] the One who "loves righteousness and justice,"[4] and who "raises those who are bowed down, protects the strangers, and upholds the orphan."[5] In short, we pray in order to feel compelled to act in a Godlike way every moment of the day.

Implementing this vision for what prayer should be is difficult, but dignifying. The program through which to achieve it is straightforward. We teach our kids how to pray and recite blessings as soon as they know how to talk. We teach them at the youngest ages that we pray in order to say "thank you" to God, and to ask God to bless us with the things we need. We need to begin teaching them that another reason we pray is to learn how to be like God.

The groundwork for this approach to prayer has been in place for a long time: The custom of placing money in a charity box during prayer is hundreds of years old. In every Jewish kindergarten class in the world, the charity box is carried around to all the children during the morning prayer. And the children dutifully and lovingly place pennies or nickels into the box. This message simply needs to be expanded and clarified.

In the end, we need to build a community that lives by the words of Rabbi Abraham Joshua Heschel: "Prayer is no substitute for action. It is rather like a beam thrown from a flashlight before us in the darkness. Prayer makes visible the right."[6] Prayer has to *matter* in order for it to be a *mitzvah*.

3. Psalm 145, verse 16.

4. From the daily Amida prayer.

5. Psalm 146, verses 8 and 9.

6. Rothschild, Fritz. *Between God and Man*. New York: The Free Press, 1959, p. 199.

To cite a further example: Orthodox law has very specific laws regarding marital sex. For approximately twelve days of each month beginning with the onset of a wife's menstruation, a married couple may not engage in any expression of physical affection whatsoever. Regarding the laws of the monthly separation as well, there is detailed information that must be taught and learned, and observance consists of many technical elements. The critical mindset change that we need to undergo is in thinking about this practice not only in terms of what it requires us to do within our own bedrooms, but also what it demands of us in the larger public discussion of sexuality and sexual ethics.

Our community generally regards the period of separation as a means through which we are regularly reminded that there is so much more to the human being than merely a body. A person is comprised of thoughts and aspirations, feelings and dreams. These are the facets of the person that we should see when we behold him or her. To focus on a person's body is to deny his or her intellectual and spiritual essence. It is denigrating to the person and offensive to God. And so we regularly step back from the body that we know most intimately, ensure that our perspective remains correct, and extrapolate from the inner dignity of our spouse to that of all other human beings. When we allow our hearts to follow our deeds and are moved by the implications of our technical observance, we will become an important voice in opposition to pornography and all forms of sexual exploitation. The defense of human dignity will become a central part of the Orthodox community's agenda. We will understand that without this commitment, we will not be completely fulfilling the laws regarding marital sex.

The same can be done even with those parts of ritual law that are seen as being highly technical and dry. Eating meat that has been "koshered" (i.e., meat from which the blood has been removed according to ritual procedure) can inspire the heart to reach a very lofty place. Moses Nachmanides the thirteenth-century Spanish sage and mystic, wrote that the reason people were originally prohibited (until the time of Noah) from eating any living thing is that "one creature possessed of a soul is not to eat another creature possessed of a soul, for all souls belong to God. The life of the man, just as the life of the animal, are all His."[7] And even when God permitted people to eat meat, God retained the spirit of this idea by prohibiting us from eating blood, "for the blood is identical with the soul, and it is not proper that one soul devour another." How vast are the implications of this *mitzvah* for our attitudes and actions toward issues of habitat destruction and animal welfare! The implications are vast if we follow the advice of The Book of Instruction, and allow our hearts to be drawn after our deeds. And this, in turn, will only occur when we think and teach with this kind of orientation. Rabbis and educators have work to do. But this work represents a big step on our return path to religious relevance.

Western Values Are Potential Religious Texts

Another critical measure of Orthodoxy's return to relevance and larger meaning will be our attitude toward ideas and values that are compatible with Orthodox thought, but which arise from outside traditional Jewish thought. We need to regularly examine these kinds of ideas for their intrinsic value and determine whether they would make us a holier and better religious community. If these tests are passed, then we have to do the creative and

7. Chavel, C. B., translator. *Ramban (Nachmanides): Commentary on the Torah*. New York: Shilo Publishing House, 1971, pp. 238–240.

educational work necessary to integrate these ideas into our religious vision and expand or change our communal behavior accordingly.

Precedents for this kind of religious development abound in Jewish history. For example, in Judaism's earlier days, polygamy and slavery were legal and recognized. On the other side of the coin, the now-common practices of bar mitzvah and Kaddish recitation by mourners simply didn't exist. (Both are medieval to late-medieval developments.) Each of these situations changed when an idea possessed of religious value and consistent with the larger thread of Jewish thought demanded that we expand or alter our practice. Monogamy, the indignity of people being treated as property, marking a child's coming of age in the synagogue, and a mourner bringing honor to a deceased parent through leading the prayers, all resonated with us, and so we took them in. This general phenomenon is by no means foreign to classical, traditional Jewish expression.

Despite this history, the last 200 years, and especially the last fifty years, have seen an abrupt about-face on this issue in the Orthodox community. The possibility of change in Orthodox religious behavior is not only resisted, it is often branded as destructive to the integrity of our religion and as a threat to its survival. Our community is still somewhat shell-shocked by the rise of modernity and the impact of the Enlightenment. The stampede toward the Jewish exit that those events wrought drove most of Orthodoxy into a defensive crouch, where it seems to be somewhat frozen. The staggering loss of scholars and institutions in the Holocaust intensified the reflexive preservationist impulse, and the severe distrust of modern ideas.

What has the cost of all this been to the Orthodox community? Already we have largely "passed" on two of the most important ideas and social developments of the last thirty years, despite the fact that they both possess religious value and are consistent with the larger thrust of Jewish thought—neither the civil rights movement nor the movement for women's rights was embraced by the Orthodox community. Jews were prominent in both struggles, but Orthodox Jews were absent. This was true in spite of the fact that the fundamental idea underlying both movements was clear. Neither skin color nor gender should determine anyone's legal rights or their worth.

This idea is not only compatible with, but has early expressions in, classical Jewish thought. The first-century sage Ben Azzai proclaimed that the verse that reiterates that "on the day that God created humankind, in the image of God He created him" (Genesis 5:1) expresses the Torah's most fundamental principle: All of us are equally endowed with the Divine spark.[8] And the sages of the *Mishnah* taught that the reason God created only one human couple is so that no human being (or race) could ever claim superior status over another.[9] Even without participating politically, the Orthodox community could have extracted the underlying principles, lent support where appropriate, and integrated the movements' insights into Orthodox life and thought. By not doing so, Orthodoxy has suffered a severe loss of relevance. Fortunately, the opportunity is still there, and there are those of us who are carefully creating a model that incorporates these values within the law and spirit of Orthodox Judaism.

I clearly recall the first time that I heard an Orthodox rabbi extol Martin Luther King, Jr. in a sermon. I was visiting the Hebrew

8. Sifra Kedoshim 45.

9. Mishna Sanhedrin 4:5.

Institute of Riverdale, N.Y., on the Saturday just preceding Dr. King's birthday. Avi Weiss, whom I knew only through his reputation of political activism for Jewish causes, was the speaker. I was thrilled when I realized that Dr. King's work and legacy would be the focus of the sermon. It had been completely outside my experience while growing up in Orthodox synagogues. After the surprise wore off, I felt embarrassed over how closed, and in this sense, how poor a community was the one I grew up in. It should not be unusual for an Orthodox rabbi to preach about Martin Luther King, Jr. His ideas amplify and enrich ours. How could we fail to embrace his religious and moral insights? Two years later, I became Rabbi Avi Weiss's assistant rabbi. Six years later I became the rabbi of my own congregation. I have never failed to devote my remarks on that special Shabbat each January to the work and memory of Dr. King.

Speaking, of course, is just a beginning. The real work is incorporating the religious imperative to recognize everyone's common humanity—the same imperative that Moses demanded Pharaoh obey—into our communal activity. It's the kind of work that will help make Orthodox Judaism matter.

The same can be said of the imperative to eliminate gender discrimination. Integrating this ideal into Orthodox thought and action is indisputably more complicated, but no less important. It is more complicated because Orthodoxy unquestionably recognizes a notion of gender *roles*. Orthodox law specifically exempts women from the performance of many of the daily rituals (such as *tefillin*, prayer at the fixed times, and daily Torah study) so that they can fulfill their roles as mothers. The roles of men and women, of fathers and mothers, are definitely not interchangeable within Orthodoxy. But it is a great mistake to believe that by endorsing gender roles Orthodoxy opposes maximizing women's spiritual opportunities.

The movement to enhance women's Jewish education has been under way for a century now. Unfortunately, there is a glass ceiling in this area in much of the Orthodox community. The study of Talmud and the Codes of Law—areas critical to the nerve center of Orthodox life—are still considered, in most Orthodox circles, off-limits to women. Nonetheless, a handful of Orthodox educational institutions are moving forward in this area of women's education. Their success will ultimately tear down one of the most important gender-discriminating walls in Orthodox life.

Even more controversial has been the effort to create prayer services for women, which meet on a periodic basis and which are led by women. Opponents of this see the creation of these prayer groups as a rejection of the Law's notion of gender roles.[10] Even the mere handling of a Torah scroll by a woman is regarded, by these opponents, as a dangerous break with tradition. But supporters understand that the prayer groups are simply a way to provide women with an important spiritual opportunity—one to which the Law could not possibly have an objection.

There are ways that the positive value of nondiscrimination can be woven into the Orthodox system, thus enriching our members, and returning us to the role of meaningful participants in the contemporary religious and ethical conversation. This part of the agenda for change is meeting particularly stiff resistance, and there is a long way to go. But every Sabbath morning, as I hand the Torah scroll to a woman in our congregation to carry through the

10. Twersky, Rabbi Meyer, "Halakhic Values and Halakhic Decisions," *Tradition*, 1998, Vol. 32, no. 3.

women's side of the sanctuary during the procession that precedes the Torah reading, I see the joy in her eyes, and I am reassured that progress will continue.

Human Dignity versus Concern for Matters of Ritual

There is one final feature in this vision for an Orthodoxy that soars beyond its present confines, one that inspires a creative, outward-looking spiritual energy and enables our community to fulfill so much more of its profound potential. It involves taking a principle of Jewish law that lives a quiet, unassuming life in the pages of the Talmud and bringing it to the fore of our religious consciousness. The principle is known as *kavod ha'briot*, which literally translates as "human dignity."

The Talmud teaches there are circumstances under which concern for human dignity overrides the law.[11] Or put another way, there are times that the law places its concern for human dignity above its concern for matters of ritual. One instance in which this sort of determination is made is the ruling that in many cases one may interrupt his or her recitation of the *Sh'ma* prayer (the central daily affirmation of our commitment to God) to respond to a friendly greeting of a passerby.[12] The thinking behind this is that the harm done to the passerby's dignity if his greeting goes unacknowledged is a weightier concern than the momentary interruption in prayer.

Another instance was played out in the Temple in Jerusalem. When people annually brought their first fruits to Jerusalem, those

11. Talmud, Tractate Menahot 37b.
12. Mishnah, Tractate Brachot.

who were literate read the prescribed formula of gratitude to God, and those who were illiterate repeated the formula word for word after the priest. When the illiterate began to stop appearing with their first fruits, embarrassed by having to repeat the formula after the priest, the sages ruled that *everyone* would repeat the formula after the priest.[13] Although this was not the ideal way to recite the blessing, concern for human dignity generated a higher value.

This *kavod ha'briot* principle need not—and should not—be thought of as merely a trouble-shooting mechanism. On its own, it must function as an autonomous religious imperative. Activities that restore dignity to fellow human beings should automatically occupy the highest rungs on the ladder of our religious behavior. They should guide how we decide to which causes we, as a community, donate our time and money. We must generate an elevated and holy protocol for how we engage, individually and communally, those with whom we disagree. This principle should influence how we view the conflict between Israel and the Palestinians. And most essentially, we must apply it to ourselves. We must demand that our religious observance create for us a life of highest dignity. It may very well require reordering our priorities, and it will certainly take a great deal of self-examination. But there isn't the slightest doubt in my mind that Orthodoxy has, and always has had, the right stuff to deliver this dignity to its adherents.

Just Doing It

It's important to get started, to seize every opportunity for forging our new mindset as it presents itself. On a Friday night a few years ago, our synagogue hosted a special service and dinner for

13. Mishnah, Tractate Bikkurim.

Jewish families who were not practicing Jewish tradition, but who were interested in learning about it. Just before we began the service, we lit the Sabbath candles, and I mentioned that by doing this we were joining an unbroken tradition among our people—a tradition that stretches back thousands of years, a tradition that highlights our commitment to peace and understanding within the home. Later, as the Sabbath dinner was winding down, one participant requested that we take special care as we clear the tables, for much of the left-over food could be wrapped and, on Sunday, brought to City Harvest, an organization that collects food for the homeless. Should not the instruments of fostering peace and well-being within our own families be shared with other families? This quickly became our new tradition. And it was evening, and it was morning, and Orthodoxy mattered.

For More Information

Habitat for Humanity, Int'l.
121 Habitat Street
Americus, GA 31709
Tel: (800) HABITAT or
   (912) 924-6935
E-mail: public_info@habitat.org
Website: www.habitat.org

The Drisha Institute of Jewish
   Education
131 W. 86th Street
New York, NY 10024
Tel: (212) 595-0307
E-mail: inquiry@drisha.org

EDAH
47 W. 34th Street, Suite 700
New York, NY 10001
Tel: (212) 244-7501

A GOOD TIME OR A GOOD LIFE? THE BLACK CHURCH IN THE TWENTY-FIRST CENTURY

Reverend Brad Ronnell Braxton

I was born in Clifton Forge, Virginia, and raised in Salem, Virginia, where my

father was pastor of the First Baptist Church. At age twenty-two, I became an ordained minister. I believe wholeheartedly in the importance of the family, and feel that one of my primary responsibilities is to be a faithful husband and good friend to my wife, Lazetta.

I was the first Rhodes Scholar in the history of Salem, a small town in southwestern Virginia. After attending the University of Virginia, I used my Rhodes Scholarship to complete a Master of Philosophy degree in New Testament studies at Oxford University, England. Now, I am a Ph.D. candidate in New Testament studies at Emory University in Atlanta, Georgia.

My sermon, "The Greatest Temptation," was recently published in The African American Pulpit, *a national journal dedicated to African-American preaching.*

In April 1995 I assumed the responsibility of senior pastor of the

Douglas Memorial Community Church, a 600-member ecumenical con-

gregation in Baltimore, Maryland. Ours is an active congregation.

Wednesday Bible study is attended by as many as 180 people each week.

Our social outreach efforts include ministries to people infected and affect-

ed by HIV/AIDS, to prison inmates and their families, and to individuals

in need of health care, clothing, and food.

As we hurl into the twenty-first century at the speed at which information travels on the Internet, the black church, a venerable spiritual and cultural institution well past its two-hundredth birthday, is alive and doing remarkably well. Much of the atrophy that has typified many mainline, predominantly white Christian denominations in the last two decades has had little effect on the black church. In black churches across the U.S., the faithful still gather in great numbers to hear the word proclaimed with rhetorical brilliance and to hear the songs of Zion sung with power and artistry.

Over the last decade, we've actually seen a substantial increase in church attendance in the black community, especially among young, upwardly mobile African-American professionals. In urban and suburban America, the up-and-coming trend is the "mega" black church with state-of-the-art classrooms, administrative offices, banquet facilities, and gymnasiums. Many of these "mega" churches have enough members to populate a small city.

Many factors contribute to this groundswell of membership. Perhaps young parents, sensing the value of continuity and tradition in raising children, are seeking again the nurture that has been a salient characteristic of black Christianity. Or maybe young African-American professionals, having bumped violently against the invisible, but nonetheless real, glass ceiling in corporate America, have come to the black church looking for the "balm of Gilead" that, as the African-American spiritual says, makes the wounded whole— even the psychologically wounded. These and a host of unnamed, and perhaps undetectable, factors are at work. But, most of all, it is the resurgence of a more charismatic style of worship in the black church that has motivated much of this interest.

It is the vibrant, exciting worship of the African-American tradition that is drawing people. People are coming—young, old, rich, poor, urban, suburban, rural—and churches are full. Yet I am concerned that congregations cultivate spiritual lives, and not simply provide energizing worship. People are coming *to* church, but what are we doing *in* church?

Worship Style versus Worship Substance

For most things in life, too much of anything, even a good thing, can be detrimental. Has our style of worship become more important than the substance of worship? Has having a "good time" in church become more important than living a good, disciplined, and empowered life before God? Has the phenomenon of stirring up feelings in church become more important than encouraging faithfulness once we are outside of the church? In the midst of all of our excitement, are we really making a difference in the world? Or just making a lot of noise?

For the black church to be relevant in the future, we must find ways together to meet a wide range of needs. The power that we experience on Sundays in our church services can be harnessed in creative ways during the week to educate and equip people for the challenges of the new century. Through serious, disciplined, spiritual instruction and innovative community outreach, the black church must seek to inform and transform every aspect of people's lives.

When religion is at its best, it should inspire integrity. In its simplest terms, this means "living with wholeness." How tragic it would be if the power of our Sunday worship experience was followed by six days of rudderless, anemic living. Perhaps our society is so broken, so fragmented, because people live such fragmented and compartmentalized lives. There is Sunday church behavior, and then there is Monday workplace behavior. If we demonstrate to people how they can lead religiously fulfilled lives not just on Sunday but everyday, maybe we can restore some integrity to American life as a whole. Excitement in church on Sunday must lead to empowerment on Monday.

The Black Church: Rediscovering the Fervor of Our Past

Anyone familiar with African-American Christianity will know that spiritual fervor has always been one of its hallmarks. This spiritual fervor, coupled with a robust hope, fanned the flames of cultural resistance that permitted African-Americans to endure slavery and segregation. Yet, it could be argued that in the post-civil rights era, some of the spiritual fervor in certain segments of African-American Christianity began to wane. Integration had exacted a substantial tax upon aspects of African-American religion.

Some African-American church leaders who participated in the civil rights movement capitulated, ironically, to the myth of white superiority. They began to feel that in order to be "acceptable," they had to adopt modes of worship and theological positions that were European. Thus, some African-American churches became uncomfortable with the very things that were African and African-American about them.

In these congregations, spiritual practices such as singing gospel music, clapping and shouting, and rhythmic vocal intonation in preaching (which in the black church is called "whooping") were no longer viewed as important, indigenous expressions of thanks to God. Instead, these practices were viewed as expendable cultural vestiges, which were beneath the sensibilities of a black bourgeoisie that was finally gaining (minimal) acceptance in white society. The problem with this spiritual capitulation to European-American culture lay not in the fact that European notions about God or practices of worship were inherently problematic or "wrong." The problem was that this capitulation seduced some African-American congregations to attempt to be exactly what they were not—white!

Thus, when some black churches adopted European religious mores instead of holding on to their indigenous practices, they jettisoned the very spiritual and cultural power that made the black church distinctive. In the quest to be acceptable, some traditional African-American churches became spiritually catatonic. The fire of black worship that had once burned red hot had been doused by the waters of cultural assimilation.

In response to the malaise that gripped some black churches in the 1970s and 1980s, African-American pastors and church leaders believed that a transfusion of spiritual power was needed. This transfusion has taken the form of the encouragement and free practice of the gifts of the Holy Spirit as enumerated throughout the New Testament and embracing again a style of worship marked by fluidity and excitement.

Over the last decade, there has been an explosion of charismatic worship in the African-American Christian tradition. Even

African-American congregations aligned with mainstream white traditions, such as the Catholic or Presbyterian churches, have infused indigenous African-American religious practices into their worship services in a large-scale way. For example, although I am a Protestant pastor, I have attended and preached in black Catholic churches. If I had closed my eyes in some of those churches, I would have thought that I was in a spirited black Baptist or Pentecostal church. Fervor has again returned to the black church. Or maybe I should say that the fervor has been uncovered for a new generation, since that fervor has always been in our tradition, even if at times it has been dormant.

Today, in many African-American churches, structured liturgies governed by printed orders of worship in bulletins are out; "praise and worship" services, where the wind of the Spirit blows where it will, are in. Piano and organ are now augmented by drumbeats and keyboards. The "shout," those powerful sessions of spiritual ecstasy, accompanied by dancing and exclamations, has been introduced to a new generation—a generation that views the civil rights movement as "ancient" history. Once again, irrespective of denominations, spiritual charisma, energy, and excitement are the order of the day in black churches.

This energy and charisma have called many young people who had turned a deaf ear back to the church. Black churches across the country are spilling over with people—especially young people. Yet, if we want to be relevant in the next century, we must be sure to build up the lives of these people with spiritual resources and skills that will enable them to negotiate the many pitfalls that life will bring to them. It is great to have so many people in church, but are we really instilling the church in them? Are we really making a difference?

Current Dilemmas of the Black Church:
We Need More "Hush" Moments

A clear warning sign that black religion and the black church might be on the verge of making more noise than making a spiritual difference came in the summer of 1997 with the explosion of the contemporary gospel song "Stomp" on the hip-hop and pop music charts. With this sacred song, the celebrated gospel artist Kirk Franklin stirred up considerable controversy. But many who were up in arms were "rioting" for the wrong reasons. More theologically conservative African-American Christians were offended because Franklin's version of this song sounded like music from a night club. And to be honest, it was "club music." The song borrowed some of its rhythmic structure from a popular "funk" band of the 1970s and 1980s named Parliament. The debate, however, about how secular this song sounds really missed the point I would like to make.

Nearly two decades ago, the revered father of Black Theology, James Cone, argued persuasively in his classic book *The Spirituals and the Blues* that in the black tradition, the spirituals and the blues, or sacred and secular songs, have never been antithetical. Instead, they are dialectical art forms and hold each other in tension. They are two sides of the same coin. The spirituals and the blues represent creative responses to oppression. The rhythmic gyrations on the dance floor in the "juke joint" on Saturday night and the spiritual "shouting sessions" in the church house on Sunday morning, more often than not, have had a similar, if not the same, genesis: They are protests against oppression and they are celebrations of life.

The deeper and more telling issue about Kirk Franklin's "Stomp" is to be found in the lyrics. The song, with its driving beat, rings out:

When I think about Your [i.e., God's] goodness it makes
me wanna stomp.... Makes me clap my hands, makes me
wanna dance and stomp. My brother, can't you see, love
got the victory?...Stomp!

Kirk Franklin's style of contemporary gospel music has brought
a whole generation of young people to the church who otherwise
might have been on the streets. However, I am using the lyrics of one
of Franklin's songs to illustrate my concern that the emphasis (or
maybe overemphasis) on overt expressions in worship may eclipse
the fullness of our rich and diverse theological heritage as Africans in
America.

I hope and pray that stomping, shouting, clapping, and the
musical intonation of black preaching will always be part of our
spiritual heritage. Yet, the best elements of the African-American
Christian tradition have also reminded us that these moments of
spiritual ecstasy were never simply ends unto themselves. Fervent
worship in our tradition has been a vehicle of deep communion
with God that has brought the necessary spiritual empowerment
and psychic release to enable us to ward off the powers that would
hinder and dehumanize us. *That* is what our churches should be
about, when we gather together in worship.

Our worship has been the dynamo that motivated us to
change the world. Worship in the black tradition has been the energy for disciplined action. The emphasis today seems to be solely on
having a *good time* in church. Whatever happened to the clarion call
to sacrifice and discipleship once the worship service is over? What
about our commitment to living *good lives?*

In the midst of our excessive celebration, are we, as the Bible
says, "putting on the whole armor of God" and preparing to combat
the many forms of the "demonic" that still confront too many black

people? Our ancestors who loved to praise God knew the value of spiritual ecstasy, but they also knew the value of disciplined reflection and sacrifice. The words of an African-American spiritual have always convicted me of the relationship between religious *empowerment* and religious *discipline:* "Every time I feel the Spirit moving in my heart I will *pray."* The anointing of the Holy Spirit in our tradition was not merely to evoke emotion or to make one feel good. The visitation of the Holy Spirit was meant to be a call to prayerful meditation so that the will of God might be executed in the life of the believer and in the world.

If the black church is to offer a relevant witness to a confused world, we must stress balance in our practice of the faith. Maybe we need to stomp and shout a little less and pray and think a little more. I have discovered that it is hard to shout and think at the same time. On occasions when I have preached in African-American congregations there has been so much excitement prior to the preaching moment that parishioners were too "worn out" to really hear and appreciate the word of God. Perhaps, sometimes when we gather we need to sit down and be quiet. The great African-American mystic Howard Thurman talked about engaging in quiet meditation so that one could watch one's self walk by.

If we stressed the importance of quiet, disciplined reflection as much as exuberant celebration, we might hear the muted voices of our African-American foreparents. In the dark night of the soul called slavery and "Jim Crowism," parishioners in black churches would sing in their revivals, "*Hush,* children, *hush* children, somebody's calling my name." These seasoned black saints of old knew that in order to hear from heaven they had to filter out earthly noise. In spite of the cracking of the overseer's whip and the inhumane slurs of the field boss, and above the shrieks of men being castrated and women being raped—above all of this demonic din, if they could just be quiet for a moment, they might hear Jesus calling them by name and telling them to fight on a little while longer.

In many black Christian congregations, you would have to search high and low to find a time when you could have a "hush moment." Sometimes our services are so emotionally oriented that it is actually hard to pray, think, and truly meditate on God's goodness. If Jesus tried to call my name in some black churches, I am sure that I would not hear him. I doubt whether His voice could compete with the organ, the tambourine, the drums, and the bass guitar. It is almost as if the louder the worship service is, the more supposedly present and active the Holy Spirit is.

Energetic, fervent worship is spiritually uplifting and empowering. Yet, I firmly believe that the Holy Spirit's primary role is not to make us feel good. The Spirit's purpose is to help us live better. The Spirit comes not so that we can make noise but that we might make a difference. Black worship is exciting, but is excitement the ultimate aim of the spiritual life? I am persuaded that spiritual transformation and human liberation are the chief priorities on heaven's agenda.

A Glimpse of the Black Church in the New Century

If the black church is to continue to be a relevant institution in the next century, we must incorporate balance in our practice of the faith.

One of my ministry colleagues in Baltimore, Dr. Frank M. Reid, III, pastor of Bethel African Methodist Episcopal Church, has spoken of the need to distinguish the *audience* from the *army* in our churches. There is so much charisma and excitement in our services that they are bound to draw audiences. Yet, there are many in the audience who have yet to be equipped for serious spiritual warfare. Our goal must not be the amassing of an audience; our goal must be the equipping of an army. Armies are equipped through patient and disciplined instruction. If we are to produce spiritually adept soldiers who are able and willing to engage in hand-to-hand combat with the demonic in its myriad forms—self-destructive lifestyles, racial and cultural xenophobia, dysfunctional families, violence, drug addiction—we must balance our love for worship with an equally enthusiastic desire to teach people how to live creative and meaningful existences.

At Douglas Church, we have taken on this task. There are many ways to worship God. Jesus said in the Gospels that we ought to love God with our hearts, our souls, and *our minds*. So during the middle of the week, we gather for serious, practical study of God's word.

On some Wednesdays, as many as 180 persons attend Bible study classes. People come in great numbers because, I think, they want more than just a good time on Sunday. People in our (and every) congregation are struggling to raise children, balance family budgets, heal fractured relationships, and fill the voids of emotional traumas. Thus, in these classes, we don't study the Bible to answer obscure historical and theological questions. We study so we are equipped to live daily for God even though we work for Caesar.

To encourage people to attend this class and make their religion more than just a Sunday affair, we made some very practical decisions about how it would operate. We deliberately placed the Bible study on Wednesday. This provides a wonderful rhythm to our worship life. After two robust worship services on Sundays, we observe "Monday Sabbath," when the church staff, the church's pro-grams, and the church building all lie fallow for twenty-four hours. By Tuesday morning, the engines of ministry are whirling again, with counseling sessions and committee meetings. But on Wednesday, we pause to worship God with our hearts, souls, and *minds* as we gather as a reading community. Many parishioners have said that Sunday "charges them up" for the week, but after two days in the hectic, often hellish world of work, they confess that their batteries need another spiritual jolt. For us, Wednesday Bible study has become the energy that renews our strength.

We who are clergy also need to be relevant today—trying to meet your needs—by making our preaching relevant. I find that when spiritual truths are packaged in straight, simple (but not sim-plistic), instructive language, people are more likely to take them home. As Warren Stewart, a noted African-American pastor, has suggested, preaching is best when it is "portable." And we want peo-ple to take the gospel home with them.

In our preaching at Douglas Church we attempt to bring Scripture to bear on everyday concerns such as finances and relation-ships. For example, discussions about money often make people very uncomfortable, yet from my experiences in counseling my members, I have discovered that money (or the mismanagement of it) is the fountainhead of many conflicts in families, especially in marriages. Therefore, instead of allowing such a practical issue to hinder so many people in my congregation, we address money head-on.

We talk as much about mortgage rates, family budgets, and life insurance policies as we do about mercy and faith. We teach a sim-ple formula for financial security: Contribute 10% to the church so that you are giving to a cause larger than yourself; save 10% so that you can accomplish your dreams for yourself; and provide for yourself off the remaining 80%. Many of our members say they have never heard preaching that talks so frankly and practically about money.

We also preach the spiritual art of forgiveness. As a pastor, I witness too frequently how the bitterness of unforgiveness eats away at human relationships like a cancer. Thus, I feel the need to address in a very practical way the importance of viewing forgiveness as a way of life and not as a fleeting, momentary act. If we can do this it will not only transform the black church, but each one of us.

Social Outreach and Social Justice Must Both Be Priorities

In order to remain relevant in the next century, the black church also must balance empowering persons for everyday living by seeking more breadth in our social outreach ministries. We have always fought for social justice. For centuries, we vigilantly led the crusade to defeat "the enemy without." That enemy has primarily been white supremacy and its many insidious implications. Yet, as we move to a new millennium, the black church must openly acknowledge that our primary foes may no longer be external, but internal. As Cornel West has rightly noted in his book *Race Matters,* many black people are currently suffocating in feelings of self-contempt and self-hatred. Consequently, so many African-Americans are turning to illicit drugs. But what seems like a life-preserver is actually a life-stealer. How will the church become a place—and a people—that overcome these problems?

Baltimore is (in)famous for its excessively high murder rate— one of the highest in the nation. A disproportionate number of murder victims and perpetrators are young black men. The black church must seek more creative ways to drive out the demons of the drug culture that are destroying our community.

Recently the mayor of Baltimore, Kurt Schmoke (who is a member of Douglas Church), hosted a meeting at our church with Baltimore clergy to discuss concrete ways that our congregations could impact life in our city. He outlined the need for more drug treatment centers in our neighborhoods. What a positive Christian witness to the world it would be if several black churches in the same neighborhood collectively sponsored a drug treatment center where people could receive a new lease on life! If we were to engage in this kind of social uplift, we would be truly carrying out the ministry of Jesus. Whenever Jesus encountered brokenness, he did not condemn it; he fixed it. When people left Jesus, they were whole.

Drug addiction is not the only malady ravaging the African-American community. HIV/AIDS, once insensitively considered to be solely a problem of the gay and lesbian community, is now affecting disproportionate numbers of African-Americans. Although African-Americans account for approximately 13% of the American population, some health officials estimate that in the year 2000, nearly 50% of the AIDS patients will be African-American. The black church can no longer stand in judgment or be silent about this issue. We must create ministries that extend the gentle hand of grace and mercy to those infected and affected by this dreaded disease.

Each year during the Christmas holidays, we partner together with Sisters Together And Reaching (STAR), a powerful, grass-roots ministry in West Baltimore specifically designed to help women and their children affected by HIV/AIDS. One of the leaders of STAR told us of their difficulty of finding a church to host their annual

Christmas fellowship. Black churches would welcome "these people" to come into their churches on Sunday, but having them in church on a Saturday for a meal was a problem.

For two years in a row, we have hosted women and their children affected by HIV/AIDS at our church for a Christmas fellowship. We share a meal and sing songs of praise, and we purchase gifts for the children. Each year, I am not sure who is ministered to the most—the women and their children or the members of our congregation. During this lunch, members of Douglas Church receive new lessons in the wonders of God's love and grace.

Jesus once declared that he had come to bring abundant life to us. Maybe teaching the skills for acquiring this abundant life should be the mandate for the black church in the new millennium. Rather than simply waiting for people to come to our churches on Sunday, we need to take the church *to* them everyday. More importantly, we must instill the values of the church in them. I am learning that when people are in church, they may have a good time, but when *the church is in them*, they will live a *good life*!

For More Information

Sisters Together & Reaching, Inc.
 (STAR)
1429 McCulloh Street
Baltimore, MD 21217
Tel: (410) 383-1903

THE JEWISH FRONTIER

Rabbi Niles Elliot Goldstein

For me, becoming a rabbi was a leap, not a step. While as I grew up, our home was kosher and our family always observed Shabbat dinner together, I was never excited by the organized Jewish community. I spent years in Hebrew  *school, but like most other young Jews I did not enjoy it and I learned little. I was very God-conscious, but not strongly connected to the institutions of public Jewish life. Not until my college years, especially after my year abroad at the Hebrew University of Jerusalem, did I begin to explore Judaism more seriously. And it was only after moving to Boston, writing a novel (and working through some inner demons), and reading the entire Torah for the first time that I realized I was being directed toward the rabbinate by forces beyond my control. I became a rabbi, not because I was attached or attracted to the apparatus of Jewish life, but because I wanted to serve my people and my God.*

My first position as a rabbi (in 1994) was as the educator for a Jewish community center. While I designed some interesting educational programs, I found that most JCC members just wanted to work out at the gym or go swim in the pool. Jewish education was just another optional "offering" of the center, and was treated as such. I moved on to serve as the assistant rabbi of a major suburban congregation. I experienced some profoundly fulfilling moments there, but I also witnessed many of the same problems that I had at the JCC. The last thing our kids wanted at four in the afternoon on a school day was more school, and the last thing our adults wanted after a hard day at the office was to drive to shul and learn about Judaism.

Since then, I've worked at two different Jewish organizations devoted to changing the mindset of the Jewish community and transforming its institutions. For two years, I was at CLAL: The National Jewish Center for Learning and Leadership, where I taught lay and rabbinic leaders. I used a wide range of Jewish material as a springboard for discussing how to create a more vibrant, compelling Judaism in our own day. Now I work as a program officer/educator at the Jewish Life Network, which is committed to religious pluralism and harmonizing the best of the Jewish tradition with the best of American culture.

I am also the voice behind "Ask the Rabbi" for Microsoft—a kind of cyber-synagogue on the Internet—and serve as a chaplain for various Federal law enforcement agencies. In addition, I am now the founding rabbi of a new, grass-roots congregation, The New Shul, in Greenwich Village, New York. My rabbinate is eclectic and atypical. What my rabbinic career will look like in twenty years is unclear. I guess it depends on what Judaism itself looks like then.

The Wilderness of Religion Today

The Kenai Peninsula juts out from the Alaskan mainland. Beyond Kenai is Kodiak Island, home to some of the largest grizzlies in North America. And beyond Kodiak are the Aleutians, a string of islands that stretch over a thousand miles across the Bering Sea. Then there is just water, ice, and emptiness. If you gaze westward from the right spot at the top of one of Kenai's mountains, and if you let your imagination drift with the wind and the waves, it can seem like you're standing at the edge of the world.

I once stood at that place. It was the summer of 1989, and in a few months I would be in Jerusalem to begin rabbinical school. What was a nice Jewish boy like me doing on a mountain in the middle of nowhere? I was seeking a home for my soul. The Jewish community, a community I would one day serve but that felt very far away at that moment, offered me little in the way of spiritual nourishment. And if I couldn't experience God within the confines of the American Jewish establishment (which seemed much more interested in building Holocaust memorials or in worrying about anti-Semitism and assimilation), I'd try to find my own Jewish path. Wherever that search took me.

I was drawn to the wilderness. I'd trekked through the

Himalayas with my father, gone on safari in Kenya, hiked through forests from Montana to Newfoundland. I'd seen nature's majesty firsthand, and I knew how it could serve as a vehicle for spiritual encounters. But all that was before I decided to become a rabbi. Now I wanted to fuse the call of the wild with the call of my faith. Where could I find a place to express myself *religiously*? I sensed that I would never be fully comfortable as a rabbi at a conventional suburban synagogue, and I suspected that I would ultimately find my spiritual home not in the Jewish mainstream, but somewhere on its fringes.

Kierkegaard refers to God as the Absolute Frontier. As I stared over the mountains at Kenai, I began to understand what he meant. It is at the boundary between the known and the unknowable that earth and heaven kiss. The frontier is the point of contact for Jacob's ladder, the place that links humanity with God. Though God may be everywhere, the concerns and distractions of our daily lives usually obstruct our vision of this cosmic truth. The wilderness helps us to clear away the clutter. The rapture I felt on that ridge—what William James calls "mystical stupefaction"—was unlike anything I'd ever experienced in a house of worship. It centered me, made me feel like I'd come home from some great journey. I didn't want the feeling to end. And as I climbed down the mountain, I knew that I had to file this memory away for life, tuck it deep into the folds of my soul. *God was real*, and I saw that, for myself as well as for other post-modern pilgrims, this spiritual insight (which could occur in the strangest of places) could provide a path away from the void of alienation and despair. I wanted to share that message with others. What I needed was a forum.

The struggle to find a home in the world of organized religion is one I haven't faced alone. Many Americans, especially those who have grown up since World War II, have turned away from the churches and synagogues of their parents and grandparents. At the cusp of the next millennium, they find little meaning in ancient liturgies and little power in unfamiliar rituals. Services seem stuffy and cold. Sermons put them to sleep. Sometimes the whole thing feels like a farce. I share many of those sentiments. Yet as a member of the clergy, my problem is a little different. For me, this isn't just about finding a spiritual community to call home. This is about my vocation, my life's work. If I don't feel fulfilled serving in one of our nation's mainstream religious institutions, then where the hell can a rabbi find a job?

We live in an age of unprecedented freedom and of multiple options. Few of us want to limit ourselves in any sphere of our lives. Even something as basic as toothpaste now comes in an astounding variety of mixtures, flavors, and containers. We have alternative medicine and alternative music—why not alternative religiosity? In post-modern America, God is no longer consigned to our traditional houses of worship. Every week, new ashrams, retreat centers, and meditation schools open. Jews and Christians discuss the Bible in study groups. Muslims study the Koran in corporate boardrooms. Religion has been deconstructed and decentralized. People today feel little discomfort about exploring their spiritual lives outside traditional venues and even outside traditional religions.

Pushing Boundaries

It is in this religious ephemera that I have tried to find my way. I've started to construct the religious life and lifestyle I know I'll need in order to heed my particular calling: a rabbinate on the edge. In a way, the decentralization of religion in America has opened up new doors for the clergy. Our career paths are no longer spelled out for us in advance. We can work in a variety of noncongregational settings and hold a range of professional positions that those who came before us could never have thought possible. There are hospital pastors, campus ministers, television preachers, and a host of other career options. None of them appeal to me. So I've tried to go a step further and take my faith to the religious *frontier*.

I am not alone. A new generation of Jewish teachers and thinkers has begun to emerge, a generation that is seeking to revitalize the traditions and institutions it has inherited even as it strives to create new ones when necessary. Many of the old structures of American Judaism are still around, such as Hadassah and the Anti-Defamation League, social action committees and fund-raising events. But something is missing. The heart and blood that gives life to all of this is getting harder for many of us to find.

The synagogue, the central Jewish institution for over two millennia, is still alive. But it is not well. Jews are voting with their feet, and synagogue affiliation and attendance are extremely low. When I served as an assistant rabbi for a large, affluent suburban New York congregation, I often found myself looking out over the pews during Friday night Shabbat services and realizing that I was almost always the youngest person there—by *decades*. Will the synagogue survive the next hundred years if young Jews no longer make it a meaningful part of their lives? This question is being addressed in different ways by different groups. For several years, the Lilly Endowment has sponsored a study called Synagogue 2000, through which a handful of innovative synagogues of various denominations around the country share what they have learned about what works—and what doesn't—in their own congregational settings.

The initial results show that certain aspects of mainstream

synagogue life no longer speak to contemporary Jews. In the 1950s and 1960s, as they moved from the cities to the suburbs, American Jews built enormous, amphitheaterlike synagogues. It was their way of showing post-war America that they had made it, that they were fully integrated into American culture and just like their Christian neighbors (on the outside at least). Synagogue architecture was formal, and the worship services reflected that same sensibility. The rabbi's pulpit was removed from the pews of the congregants; his sermons (there were no women rabbis yet) were lofty and cerebral; the liturgical music was operatic, there was frequently a choir, and people sat passively through the service except for responsive readings in English.

Jews today recoil from such formality and distance. They want warmth and proximity, emotion and participation—in their architecture, in their services, and in their clergy. They don't want a show. They want a *community*. In some of the more successful synagogues, congregants, not professionals, sometimes preach the sermons, chant the Torah portions, conduct the services. Lines between clergy and laity, while not erased, are more relaxed. Spirituality, informality, and multiple options are key features of this revitalized religious life: accessible music that we can all sing, *chavurot* (small prayer groups) within the larger congregation that all can join, a religious experience that touches our souls as much as our minds. By adopting these approaches and attitudes, the synagogue will not die out. Instead, it will be rejuvenated and transformed.

Another mainstay of Jewish life in need of revitalization is the United Jewish Appeal (now the United Jewish Communities), the primary fund-raising arm of American Jewry. For decades, the various UJA chapters around the country have raised hundreds of mil-

lions of dollars for different causes, predominantly within the
Jewish community. They have helped Jewish community centers,
social service agencies, and homes for the aged. And for the last fifty
years, since the creation of the State of Israel in 1948, the UJA has
sent the majority of its annual gifts to the Jewish State to aid its
growth as a strong and modern nation. But now that Israel is an
existential fact, now that it is financially stable and politically
accepted by the world community, the situation has changed. The
most pressing problem facing world (and especially American)
Jewry at the end of the twentieth century is no longer physical survival, but the religious and cultural literacy of its members, the
preservation, practice, and perpetuation of the very traditions and
values that gave birth and meaning to the Jewish community in the
first place.

The UJA has begun to recognize this problem and to redefine
its mission. It has started to turn inward, to shift its priorities
toward Jewish identity and education. One such initiative that UJA's
New York chapter has created is its Continuity Grants, which are
awarded to innovative programs that focus on providing attractive
Jewish options to underserved populations, such as singles, young
couples and families, college students, new immigrants, and the
unaffiliated. Without their participation, organized Jewish life will
continue to falter and Judaism will become a hollow shell of what it
could be. While supporting Israel and sustaining nursing homes are
vital, necessary activities, these kinds of commitments will never be
enough to instill Jewish identity or to educate our people about
their heritage. For too long we have let Jews think that sending a
check to the UJA was a sufficient expression of their "Jewishness."
We need to push them now to learn about their faith—and to live
it. We must help them uncover the Jewishness inside of them, and

teach them that it is only after Judaism has been *interiorized* that it can truly bloom.

Immersion Experiences Are Vital to Jewish Life

Times have changed radically in the 2,000 years since the early rabbis created the Judaism that has been handed down to us, in ever-modified form. Times have also changed remarkably since the beginning of the century that is about to end. Sometimes the revivification of old institutions is not enough. Sometimes we need to create *new* ones, fresh models of religious life that connect more deeply with the hearts and souls of our people. When the Romans destroyed the Second Temple in Jerusalem in 70 C.E., they demolished not only a building but a way of life that had been practiced for centuries. Rather than succumb to defeat, the early rabbis, led by Judah the Prince and his disciples at their academy in Yavneh, reshaped Judaism. The biblical religion that had been based on temples, priests, and sacrifices was transformed into a spiritual system centered around synagogues, rabbis, and prayers. This brave and ingenious response saved Judaism from receding into oblivion. Many contemporary Jews think that a similar response is called for in our post-Holocaust, post-modern world, an age as fragmented and wounded as any other. But how do we create new Jewish institutions in an era that is profoundly anti-institutional? How do we design new religious paths in a period that is so ambivalent about organized religion?

Until the close of this century, most mainline religious denominations (such as Presbyterianism, Methodism, and Reform Judaism) favored creed over ritual, universal concerns over their own particular interests. Though each denomination might have its own belief system, they all worshiped the same God and were all devoted to the same moral ideals. This spiritual "melting pot" idea has failed. Americans have fled in droves from their churches and synagogues. One of the reasons that New Age groups and fundamentalist movements have been so successful is that they understand this failure, which is ultimately a failure of some of the core principles of modernity itself. Rather than concentrating on dogma and theology, they focus on behavior; rather than trying to use rationality as the gateway to religion, they use emotion and spirituality; rather than minimizing a religious tradition's distinctiveness (even otherness), they celebrate it. Despite the discomfort that many of us feel with some of their spiritual practices (such as sweat lodges and prayer crystals), these groups are filling a void—and drawing in followers—by providing a tactile, even primal power that the cerebralism and detachment of mainstream religion cannot offer. They also create communities that are bonded not by social convention or ideology, but by joy and shared experience.

Like many other American Jews, I'm convinced that many of the models we are currently using to promote Jewish literacy and identity don't work. Sunday school, sisterhood luncheons, buying a tree for Israel from the Jewish National Fund, even an occasional prayer service—none of these things, which are intermittent and which inevitably separate our "Jewish lives" from our everyday lives, have been truly effective at attracting and connecting Jews (especially younger Jews) to their Judaism. This compartmentalization has been more of an obstacle than a catalyst for spiritual revitalization. The answer does not lie in separation and detachment, but in *immersion.*

Our souls must be bathed in their Jewishness. They must be enveloped by their spiritual heritage if it is ever going to "stick" in them and become anything more than an appendage or ornament to their more mundane lives. They must also be freed from the ideologies and denominationalism that constrain their spiritual explorations. The organization where I currently work—Jewish Life Network—is devoted to these goals. Its president, Rabbi Yitz Greenberg, and chairman, Michael Steinhardt, both believe that for Judaism to grow and thrive in postmodern America, it must be experiential, multidenominational, and embody the best of both Jewish and American culture. It is too late—and not desirable—to retreat to the shtetls in eastern Europe from which most of our ancestors came. But it is high time that the Jewish community created models of Jewish life that incorporate our new knowledge about the successes and failures of modern organized religion.

One of the projects that we are now trying to develop is a Jewish retreat center. The center would provide a total Jewish environment for its participants, a setting and structure that would immerse every person there in a Judaism that is not just studied but *lived*. The schedules, symbols, activities, and food would all be linked to Judaism. The fellowship that is created will be a Jewish fellowship. While the experience might only last a weekend or a week, it would be powerful enough (and it could be repeated often enough) to transform lives. The retreat center would offer a dynamic, attractive alternative to the traditional institutions of Jewish life. It would not be associated with a particular movement but with the values of pluralism. A prayer center, where different services (Orthodox, feminist, egalitarian) could take place in different rooms at the same time under one roof, would be the center's spiritual heart. For ideological or aesthetic reasons, not all Jews would feel comfortable praying together, but they could all certainly share wine and challah after worship as a single, supportive religious community.

The long-lasting effects of the warmth, informality, and powerful religious experiences that the center would provide are key elements that have worked elsewhere. Organizations like CLAL: The National Jewish Center for Learning and Leadership and the Wexner Heritage Foundation have retreats at the core of their programs; the *chavurah* and Jewish renewal movements, most of the Jewish youth movements, the *ba'al teshuvah* outreach groups, many synagogues, even the UJA, all use retreats to inspire and educate Jews. It is no secret that this idea works; the mystery is why the American Jewish community as a whole has not yet developed easily accessible, first-class retreat facilities around the country so it could stop relying on improvised locations at hotels, conference centers, and camps. Only a dedicated space (like the Brandeis-Bardin Institute in Los Angeles, the classic example of a Jewish retreat center) can build the reputation that is necessary to attract new participants and lead to repeat experiences.

Another model of the Jewish immersion experience that is related to retreat centers is the summer camp. Study after study has shown how successful Jewish camps have been in inculcating Jewish identity. Many of today's rabbis and communal leaders are products of camping experiences. Few settings are as effective at intertwining meaningful Jewish experiences with exciting secular ones (such as a camp-wide Shabbat celebration or a Maccabiah sports day). This is an insight shared by others. A recent *New York Times* article pointed out that many American immigrant groups, like Muslims, Sikhs, and Hindus, are developing camps of their own in order to fend off assimilation in their own communities. But many Jewish camps cannot compete qualitatively with some of the better, secular camps. And the good ones are expensive. There are also just not enough Jewish camps in America to meet the demand for them. One new organization, the Foundation for Jewish Camping, is trying to confront these issues. It plans to award grants to camps (of all Jewish denominations) so they can improve their facilities and programming, attract talented staff, provide scholarships to those campers in financial need, and aid in the construction of new camps.

One Jewish educational model that is almost universally regarded as a problem is Hebrew school. Several factors hamper Hebrew schools' ability to transmit Jewish knowledge and inspire young Jews to live fuller Jewish lives. First of all, Hebrew school is the antithesis of a spiritual immersion experience. For one or two afternoons per week (and sometimes including Sunday morning), children—already tired and hungry from their regular classes at school—show up for a couple of hours of religious instruction. Years later, most retain little or nothing of their Jewish education, and most have profoundly negative associations with Judaism and Jewish life.

An answer to this problem is the Jewish day school movement. It is a "movement" in the sense that it crosses denominational lines, that it is rooted in a recognition that current models of Jewish schooling seem to have failed and that a new one must be pursued vigorously if serious Jewish education and identity can occur in our young people. This is a tough pill for American Jews (who have historically been proponents of public schools and enjoy exposing their children to multicultural experiences) to swallow. But it is clear that an early immersion in Jewish education and culture is a powerful way to transmit Jewish knowledge and ingrain Jewish identity in young minds and souls. There is simply more Jewish content, more Jewish time, more Jewish atmosphere, and more Jews in a Jewish day school. No supplementary school can possibly make

Judaism so integral to its everyday pulse. Orthodoxy already has an extensive day school network, but such a system must be encouraged in the more liberal movements. Groups like the Partnership for Excellence in Jewish Education are making strides in this area by supporting such schools.

The essential component of an "immersion" approach to Jewish life is raw experience. Until recently, Jewish programming has often focused on the intellect. Adult education courses, sermons, liturgies—all these appealed to our reason and tried to convince us of the *truth* of Jewish beliefs, values, and religiosity. This approach was misguided. Human beings do not always do what they know they should do, and human knowledge comes from a variety of places, not just from ideas and words. An *experiential* element is critical to revitalizing the Jewish community, for it is experience more than perhaps anything else that informs our sensibilities and shapes our lives. A person must fall in love in order to truly understand it. We must first taste an apple before we can describe its sweetness. And Jews must experience Judaism (not just read or hear about it) in order to fully appreciate its power or grasp its application to their lives. For Judaism to be inspiring, for it to take root in our souls, we must immerse ourselves in it and live in it in tangible, concrete ways. Jewish leaders need to balance the Judaism of the brain with the Judaism of the body and soul. We must meet Jews where they are, not where we think they ought to be.

One example of this approach to Judaism and Jewish education is the outdoor adventure trip. Jews by the thousands (particularly younger, unaffiliated ones) have flocked to the various outfitters in the adventure travel industry, a rapidly growing field that provides exciting, challenging, life-changing experiences to anyone willing to "rough it" in the wild. In recent years, many people have come to see this as a golden opportunity: a captive audience of young Jews having an experience of a lifetime without any Jewish content or framework built into it yet.

Several different Jewish groups around the country have tried to fill this void. By combining the challenges of an Outward Bound-type physical adventure with informal Jewish education, they have created an approach to Jewish life that would have been unheard of just a generation ago. With names like Burning Bush Adventures (which is in Vermont), Endangered Spirit and Steppin' Out (located in Chicago), and Jewish Adventure Travel, which I founded with Bob Greenbaum (and which is based in California and New York), these grass-roots, often shoestring operations reach out to Jews who want to harmonize Judaism's teachings with nature and physical challenge. What does Judaism have to say about community, teamwork, and trust? Learn about it while the only thing that separates you from the desert floor a hundred feet below is the help of a total stranger at the other end of your rope. How does Judaism tell us to confront our fears and overcome obstacles? It will never be clearer than during a cold, grueling dog-sledding expedition in northern Minnesota.

The power of these adventure experiences—a power that goes beyond reason alone—can transmit Judaism and imprint it in the souls of the participants. These experiences also help break the negative associations with Judaism that many Jews have carried with them since Hebrew school days; it replaces these with exhilaration, joy, friendship, and personal and collective triumph. I know the spiritual power of nature firsthand: My own experience hiking through Alaska opened my eyes to the realm of the transcendent in a transformative way, and helped prepare me for the rabbinate. It was my Sinai. These revelations, great and small, should be accessible to every one of us.

Reaching Out to Jews at the Edge

The new models for Jewish life in America that I have described (retreat centers, summer camps, day schools, adventure travel experiences) are *public* ones. They can and should be replicated from community to community. The key to all of them is that they are all-enveloping and multi-denominational. There will always be Reform camps and Orthodox yeshivas, but if we want to apply any of these models to the majority of Jews in this country— to people who are detached from the public institutions of Judaism and who couldn't care less about ideology or theology—our leaders must focus more on the structural and experiential issues of its projects and less on particular creeds. For Judaism to be robust, dynamic, and attractive in twenty-first century America, it has to expand its tent to envelop a wide range of models for Jewish life and education—models in which all Jews are made to feel welcome and at home.

I have tried to create a rabbinate that embraces and embodies these notions—but on a private scale. Although I have worked in congregations, which is the traditional post for a rabbi, I have also gone out of my way to explore some new and unusual alternatives. One part of my rabbinate that reflects this emphasis on outreach is my work on the Internet. I am the rabbi of a *cyber*-synagogue. In many ways, what I do for Microsoft is starkly different from the work of a pulpit rabbi. For one thing, this congregation is open twenty-four hours a day. If anyone has a pressing concern or question, all he has to do is leave it on "Ask the Rabbi" and he'll get a response from me long before most of my colleagues who work in congregations would even receive the message. While you can't perform a *bris* or conduct a funeral over the Internet, for many people that lack of focus on ritual is itself an enticement. Those turned off by organized religion but open to spiritual issues often find themselves drawn to our section of cyberspace.

In other ways my work is surprisingly similar to that of a conventional cleric. My "lectern" may be made of wires instead of wood, but I still use it to preach my sermons. I might not teach adult education classes to congregants while they're seated around a table, but I talk about the Jewish tradition with Internet users every day (and intermittently conduct live discussions on various topics in our Judaism chat room). I may not have an actual office for private counseling or confidential conversation, but I do have an e-mail address for those situations where discretion or personal, one-on-one communication is required. I've led some people through the mourning process and helped others trace their religious genealogies. And though I didn't do the matchmaking at a congregational picnic, three of our assistants met their future spouses online.

Most of the users I encounter have problems with religious practice. They are often nonobservant and find little meaning in ancient rituals or indecipherable liturgies. But just the fact that they are in the newsgroup is spiritually significant. They, like many other Americans, are yearning for something that will enrich their lives and root them in a spiritual community.

Historically, religion has been defined by boundaries and parameters, distinctions in beliefs, holy books, practices, calendars. The Internet has no boundaries. I once asked our users what they thought about the notion of creating new rituals that would speak more to their own experiences. One woman suggested a liturgy to mark menopause. A father wanted to construct a ceremony for sending his daughter off to college. A teenager argued for a new blessing to be recited at the time of a boy's first wet dream. I didn't like all the ideas, but I loved the free, uncensored exchange of views, an exchange that would have been extremely difficult outside the Internet.

In an age when religion has been deconstructed and decentralized, few media reach as many potential "congregants" as the Internet. We never have to look for extra chairs to accommodate overflow crowds. Millions of believers can join us from anywhere in the world. The anonymity that a virtual religious community confers encourages people to speak more candidly. But in the absence of face-to-face encounters, relationships between members of a virtual community will always be limited. Nothing will ever be able to replace the embrace of another human being or the feeling of families at prayer. Contact is not communication. We may all be created in the image of God, but only the shadows of those images will be visible online. The Internet is a mixed blessing. It draws people together at the same time that it distances them. It expands the horizons of religion while collapsing its moorings and traditions.

Another aspect of my rabbinate that fits into the category of outreach is my "missionary" work. I'd heard many exotic tales over the years from my Jesuit friends about their missions to places like India and Africa. Since the Jewish community didn't offer those kinds of opportunities to its rabbis, I decided to create my own missions to help Jews in regions as remote and underserved as possible. The first of these took place in the summer of 1993 when I went to the new, post-Soviet republics of Kazakstan, Kyrgyzstan, and Uzbekistan. I led worship services, gave lectures on Jewish history and thought, and distributed books and medicine that I'd brought with me from the States. I gathered data on Jews who were trying to emigrate. I also did some pastoral work, visiting the sick and elderly as well as trying to console the bereaved. Much of it was similar to what a rabbi does in most mainstream congregations in America, but for me the context was everything. Most of these Jews knew next to nothing about their heritage and spiritual traditions. Unlike many members of the American Jewish community, these Jews didn't take their Judaism for granted. Almost anything I taught them, anything *religious,* was new to them. God was beginning to break through the Iron Curtain. It was religion in the raw—the revelation at Sinai, the view from Kenai.

I returned to the former Soviet Union three years later. The Caucasus region was just beginning to calm after several years of intense violence: war between Azerbaijan and Armenia, civil strife in Georgia, and bitter fighting in and around the breakaway Russian republic of Chechnya. I traveled through Kabardina-Balkaria and North Ossetia, remote provinces at the southern edge of Russia. Much of my activity was similar to what I had done in Central Asia: distributing medicine, books, and religious articles, and teaching, counseling, and collecting information on those who were trying to leave and to begin better lives somewhere else. Most of the Jews I met in Nalchik (the capital of Kabardina-Balkaria) wanted to emigrate. Inflation was out of control. Kidnappings and extortion schemes were rampant. The war in Chechnya was omnipresent: There were checkpoints everywhere, especially on the highways, and bomb scares were not uncommon. The Jews felt particularly vulnerable. Though they'd lived with their Muslim neighbors for years, people were looking for scapegoats. As a small religious minority in a time of rapidly rising nationalism and economic turmoil, the Jews of Nalchik felt like easy targets.

The Jews in North Ossetia were altogether different. European in appearance and background, their presence in the Caucasus went back only several decades, when Stalin had sent them south—along with other ethnic groups—to try to foster their assimilation into the new Soviet culture. Vladikavkaz is the capital of the Ossetian nation, a Christian, pro-Russian island in a sea of hostile Muslim republics. The Russian army has used this to its advantage, transforming North Ossetia into a staging ground for its troops in their war with Chechnya, which is just across the border. Despite all these problems, the majority of Jews I met in Vladikavkaz wanted to stay put. The only Jewish organizations they'd heard from over the years had offered to help them—but only if they'd move to Israel. These people weren't interested in being shuttled anywhere. This was their home. Those who had jobs liked them: Many were scientists, physicians, academics, and teachers. They needed help, but they wanted it on their terms. They wanted to develop their *own* communities there. They wanted to build a synagogue and a school. They wanted to be, as they phrased it, "normal Jews."

In addition to my work as an Internet rabbi and self-styled Jewish missionary, I am also a chaplain for Federal agents. Entering the world of cops and criminals is not a common career move for a rabbi. But I felt an almost instinctive attraction to the law enforcement community. Its fundamental mission—the pursuit of justice—seemed to mesh perfectly with one of the central tenets of the Jewish faith, since it was the prophet Isaiah who declared: "Justice, justice shall you pursue!"

The trick to any successful ministry is to meet people where they are—and cops tend to congregate in some pretty dark places. I've counseled agents in pubs, discussed marital problems in interrogation rooms. I wear a beeper. When an agent's in trouble (which could mean anything from being involved in a shooting to contemplating suicide), it goes off. Sometimes an agent just wants to meet for a beer and schmooze. Agents tend to keep their problems to themselves. They're afraid department shrinks will inform on them to their supervisors. Law enforcement officers as a whole are distrustful and often have a dim view of human nature and the world—they deal with society's underbelly on a daily basis. Losing faith in God in their line of work is an occupational hazard.

One day I drove with two Drug Enforcement Administration agents through sections of the south Bronx that looked like they'd been strafed by gunfire. I saw a lot of people going about their everyday lives, but I also saw dealers, junkies, and prostitutes. It was grim. A decade ago, the agents told me, the main drugs on the street were depressants, like heroin and marijuana. Now they were stimulants like crack cocaine and methamphetamines. Violence had increased exponentially. Weapons were everywhere. Crack and crystal meth were ripping the guts out of entire neighborhoods. "Where is God in all this?" they asked me. It wasn't the view from Kenai. It was hard to see beauty and order while working in a landscape that was so scarred by desperation and poverty. But the fact that they raised the question meant that a door had opened, that a religious dialogue between a rabbi and a couple of G-men who had not stepped into a church or synagogue in years could begin.

A Tradition in Need of Change

Ours is an age of intense spiritual yearning. Yet many people who need spiritual guidance the most aren't always the ones who attend a church or a synagogue. So I go to them. Because I seek the frontier myself, I understand those who stand on religion's periphery, on the edge of faith. Not all of them are ready or willing to enter the confines of organized religion, with its rites, rituals, and ceremonies. The experience I had at Kenai, though, the message that God was real, transcends any house of worship. If God is really the Absolute Frontier, then it makes sense that the view from the edge—whether the technological, geographical, or societal one—would afford us an especially privileged vantage point for discovering this religious truth.

It is at faith's frontiers, through the revitalization of old religious models and the creation of new ones, that Judaism stands the best chance of survival. Our clergy, programs, and institutions need to meet people where they are—before we even think about helping to bring them to where we believe they ought to be. Baby boomers, who currently hold most of the leadership positions in the Jewish community and thus much of the power, have made "spirituality" the buzzword of their tenure. But personal spirituality is not enough. If we focus excessively on the desires and needs of the individual, ignoring the centrality of community and eroding the sense of obligation and responsibility so vital to our religious tradition, Judaism as a demanding but deeply fulfilling way of life will degenerate into simple self-help. Its foundations will crumble under the weight of spiritual narcissism.

There is no formula for engendering Jewish identity or inspiring American Jews to live fuller Jewish lives. Still, if we are secure and self-confident enough to admit them, we can learn from our mistakes and get beyond them. We have seen what a failure the compartmentalization of Judaism has been, how separating it from our daily lives will lead to its atrophy and ultimate disappearance. We know that institutional Judaism has been dull and overly cerebral. We understand that the fear of assimilation and the threat of anti-Semitism do little to motivate this generation of Jews to affiliate with the Jewish community or to behave Jewishly. And we have observed how spirituality without communal and religious commitment leads to self-absorption.

We should not hold on to institutions and strategies if they no longer work. If they—like the synagogue and federation system—can be revitalized and made to speak to today's Jews, let us get to work. If not, let's have the strength to abandon them and move on. What we need today are powerful and creative immersion experiences, models for Jewish education and Jewish living that are exciting, substantial, accessible, and free of the wasted energy of denominationalism. We need to turn on the disaffected among us and tap into those who still stand at a distance from their heritage. Modernity is in its death throes. Judaism, like other American religions, has no choice but to take a new shape as we step into this new era.

For More Information

The Brandeis-Bardin Institute
1101 Peppertree Lane
Brandeis, CA 93064
Tel: (805) 582-4450

Burning Bush Adventures
Tel: (802) 442-9645

CLAL: The National Jewish
    Center for Learning and
    Leadership
440 Park Avenue South, 4th Floor
New York, NY 10016
Tel: (212) 779-3300

Endangered Spirit
653 W. Barry, Suite 2F
Chicago, IL 60657
Tel: (773) 244-9625

The Foundation for Jewish
    Camping
6 E. 39th Street, 10th Floor
New York, NY 10016
Tel: (212) 279-2288

Jewish Adventure Travel
69-844 Highway 111, Suite H
Rancho Mirage, CA 92270
Tel: (800) 998-7585

Jewish Life Network
6 East 39th Street, 10th Floor
New York, NY 10016
Tel: (212) 279-2288

The Partnership for Excellence in
  Jewish Education
678 Massachusetts Avenue, Suite
  305
Cambridge, MA 02139
Tel: (617) 491-9190

Steppin' Out
1936 N. Clark, Suite 23
Chicago, IL 60614
Tel: (773) 509-8595

THEOLOGICAL DEMOCRACY IN THE LIBERAL CHURCH

Reverend Stephanie R. Nichols

I grew up in Winchester, Massachusetts, went to Dartmouth College, and double-majored in mathematics and religion. I believed, until about May of my senior year, that math was the practical choice that would send me

into a career, while comparative religion was much more interesting than useful. One day, however, a corporate recruiter came to campus to lure technically minded seniors into analyst positions at her company. Listening to her pitch, I felt absolutely nothing, aside from a small pit forming somewhere in my gut. My career plans vanished in that moment. With no idea what I would do instead, I left the room.

Within months, the idea of seminary emerged. I had contemplated it briefly during my youth group days in the Unitarian Universalist church in Winchester. Now it recurred with real energy. In 1984, I moved to

Berkeley, California, to attend Starr King School for the Ministry, the Unitarian Universalist school of the Graduate Theological Union, a consortium of theological schools.

I had no doubts about ministry as a career, but I did feel some reluctance about taking a straight-line path into the parish. So I took a leave of absence in 1986 and walked across the United States with the Great Peace March for Global Nuclear Disarmament. What an adventure! I met wonderful friends, saw the nation's cornfields in fifteen-mile increments, and did it in the name of a cause I believed in. The Peace March led to an opportunity to walk from St. Petersburg to Moscow in Russia, which led to an opportunity to bring some Russian young adults to the United States for speaking tours and travel.

In 1988, these experiences translated into a position in community ministry at the UU Peace Network in Philadelphia. My two commitments, peace and ministry, came together. It was a good job, but the office was about to close down and I was feeling the call to a local parish at last.

I served in the UU church in Fresno, California from 1993 to 1997. I learned a lot about churches and people there. I also learned that to be most effective in the church, you must sink roots deeply into the local soil, and that the place I most wanted to do that was "back home" in New England.

Here in Massachusetts, I have been UU chaplain at Wellesley College. Religious identity is more important to students than most people know.

In May 1998, I received a call to First Parish in Framingham, Massachusetts. I am hopeful that this will be a long and satisfying ministry.

Love Is the Doctrine

Each Sunday as I step into the pulpit to lead worship, I know that I serve in a healthy, vital local church. Up to 300 voices sing the opening liturgy and speak in unison a covenant that begins, "Love is the doctrine of this church." From the perspective of this congregation, liberal religion is alive and well. Even as many mainstream religious groups have been suffering decline, Unitarian Universalism has seen a period of steady growth. Why might this be? Here are some thoughts gleaned from the first decade of my career.

Our congregations succeed to the extent that we honor:

 - the integrity of each individual's spiritual search;
 - the life circumstances of the people walking through our doors;
 - the histories of Unitarianism, Universalism, and post-1961 merged Unitarian Universalism;
 - the story of our own unique congregation;
 - what makes people happy to be in church, and what gets in the way.

In my own work, I notice that if I let go of any one of these emphases, I immediately become less effective. I am responsible for tending both to individuals and to an institution. Attention to people without regard for the institution eventually leads to a lack of identity and focus in the church; overemphasis on the institution while letting pastoral care and the needs of real human beings lapse eventually leads to Sunday morning services with no one in attendance. Careful attention to both, however, gives people a sense of being cared for and inspired, as well as being part of something enduring and important and value-centered.

Unitarian Universalists are organized with a system of congregational polity, the "bottom up" structure first established by the Cambridge Platform in 1648. This means that our congregations are related to one another by association, but not bound by the higher authority of a bishop or central office. The staff at Unitarian Universalist Association headquarters in Boston may make suggestions and requests to local congregations, but do not hold authority over them. Local congregations govern themselves, fund themselves, and call and ordain their own ministers.

Consequently, local identity is particularly important to us. A church-shopper is likely to find tremendous variation in character and style from one UU congregation to another, and it is not uncommon to hear a newcomer say, "I tried several churches, and this is the one where I feel most at home." Now that I have served in several congregations, I am more convinced than ever that "all religion is local." First Parish in Framingham is what it is because of its 300-year history: a healthy, spirited, relatively large congregation with excellent music and religious education.

All religion is also relational, whether the relationship is between one person and another, or between a person and God. The way we transform lives is not by issuing proclamations or setting policy; it is by bringing people together, respecting them fully, and inviting them to become their best selves. Sometimes it is as simple as helping them to stop shooting themselves in the foot, pointing the way toward a free and full life. Sometimes our task, as the saying goes, is "to comfort the afflicted and afflict the comfortable," to reassure and challenge and inspire. Sometimes it is as stark as providing a place to go when it's time to die.

Quiet conversations between clergy and parishioners happen every day, in all kinds of settings. In my ten years of ministry, people have spoken to me about the widest range of concerns: battles with cancer and a variety of chronic and terminal illnesses; unhappy marriages and relationships; struggles with sexual identity; vocational problems; the challenges of raising difficult children, caring for aging parents, being the aging parents, and coping with loss; battles to overcome addictions to alcohol, drugs, tobacco, and food; problems with abusive partners and relatives; problems encountering prejudice; grief of every kind; efforts to maintain religious identities in interfaith marriages; struggles with choosing a different religious path than the rest of the family; searches for God; making preparations for death.

These conversations take place in my office, on walks in the woods, in homes, and in hospital rooms. They take place in the hallway outside coffee hour after church, in the aisles of the supermarket, and over a cup of tea at the bookstore.

Important moments happen in planned and unplanned ways every day in the life of a church. We must cultivate these intimacies in order to remain a vital place for spiritual growth in the next century.

Lives of Holy Moments: Ministry Happens in Mundane and Inconspicuous Ways

A woman sits down and tells me something deeply personal about herself. I listen, respond, sit with her while she cries, reassure her she's not alone. I am the face of the church at that moment: We are here when she needs somewhere to turn, and I feel privileged to be hearing her story. It is a holy moment.

It is newsletter day and the office staff is overworked even before a phone call brings them another "urgent" assignment. The administrator makes two phone calls and in minutes, three volunteers agree to come in and help. Within an hour, a cheerful work party is folding, stuffing, labeling, talking and laughing, and the stress has vanished. A mundane scene, but the generosity of the volunteers makes it another holy moment.

On Saturday afternoon I am wrestling with a sermon on forgiveness. Staring at the computer screen and hearing the clock tick, I feel that creeping insecurity that haunts all clergy at one time or another: What can I possibly say that will make a bit of difference to anyone? It is perfectly clear to me why forgiveness has vexed humanity since the beginning of time, and who am I to climb up in the pulpit in a robe and be a spiritual leader? And then miraculously, the kernel of an idea presents itself as a gift from heaven, and by midnight I have a sermon. For just a few moments the next morning, the congregation is totally listening to me, and I know why I am there.

There are many other moments in this week, of course. Newcomers want information about the church; there are committee meetings and staff meetings and preparations for the upcoming pledge campaign. There is an evening class for adults that I lead and a gathering of the local interfaith clergy association to attend. There are pastoral telephone calls and a visit to the hospital and a big pile of mail to sort. Some of these things feel immediately gratifying and worthwhile; others fall more in the category of "I hope this proves to be a good use of my time someday." The business of transformation, of myself as well as those who come to church in search of something deeper in life, happens ever so gradually, and sometimes in the most mundane and inconspicuous ways.

The Church Is a Place for Seekers

I love the church because, a few guilt-driven and hopeless martyr types notwithstanding, it is a place where people come by choice, not by requirement. I am sure this is true for all of us in local congregations, but it is particularly true for Unitarian Universalists— the whole enterprise works because people are there voluntarily. They want to give their time and money and talent, they want a peaceful worship hour in their week, they want quality religious education for their children, and they want a community of like-minded seekers. I suspect they also hope that one day, if they really need it, the church will be there for them in a spiritual crisis. These wants are deep, and consequently people will do remarkable things to sustain the church. As minister, I witness their acts of quiet generosity all the time. I meet some of the finest people I could ever want to know, I get a real belly laugh from somewhere almost every day, and there are many moments in the life of the church that move me deeply.

One December day, a woman I didn't know requested a brief appointment. She was a newcomer to the church. She sat down and handed me a plain envelope. "I hope you will use this," she said, "to make someone's holiday happier. When I was eighteen, my parents divorced and we had no money. Our minister quietly handed my mother an envelope from an anonymous donor, and it allowed us to have a real Christmas. I am twenty-four now, and I want to return the favor." After she left, I opened the envelope and found hundreds of dollars in cash. I felt the tears well up. An experience like that every now and then makes up for a fair number of martyrs and petty hassles and budgetary woes.

Now, these are scenes that could have taken place in any congregation. They are not unique to Unitarian Universalism, nor did they happen to me because I am a "younger" minister. They are, however, delightful and moving scenes that suggest the possibilities for organized religion in contemporary America.

Those who are unchurched today may think primarily of long, boring sermons, bad potluck suppers, and socially out-of-touch clergy when they think about religion. (Or, they may simply think about how structured and busy the rest of the week is, and how much they treasure slow Sunday mornings with coffee and the *New York Times*.) But what I see, as someone who is paid to be at church for two services, two coffee hours, and an after-church meeting or two every week, is a vibrant, caring community that respects and speaks to all ages, and sends people back out into the world glad they were there and with a little perspective for the week ahead.

Theological Freedom Is a Religious Alternative

That said, I also see some unique features of Unitarian Universalism that may have let us adapt particularly well to the changing needs of American churchgoers. These are qualities we must cultivate. First, we have extraordinary theological freedom. As a noncreedal church, we do not require adherence to any dogmatic statements of faith. We do, however, require assent to the *process* of living a faithful life. We understand the limitations of words: The vocabulary a person uses to describe ultimacy is of necessity inadequate, and all statements about God are metaphorical. Theological perspectives also change over the course of a lifetime, as people experience particular joys, sorrows, and dilemmas. It is not unusual for a person to have periods of theism, agnosticism, enthusiasm, and doubt; periods of comfort and certainty with a particular theological view, and periods of shift or upheaval. We assume and embrace this kind of evolution.

This freedom presents opportunities as well as pitfalls. It is easy, in a Unitarian Universalist church, to bring your questions and your deep searching to our house of worship. It is less easy to sink deeply into any one metaphor for the holy, because it won't necessarily be a vocabulary shared by the person in the next pew.

Another feature of Unitarian Universalism that may help us adapt readily to the current American religious scene is that we are accustomed to our role as "religious alternative." At a time when some mainstream religious groups have to redefine themselves in order to stay relevant, we are taking advantage of our reputation as "a different kind of church." People come to us specifically because they hear we "aren't like other churches." This, too, provides an opportunity and a pitfall. On the positive side, people come to us with open minds, ready to be pleased with something flexible and new. The pitfall, however, is with those who come to us more sure of what they don't want than what they do. Here are the kinds of things we typically hear from newcomers:

"I was raised Protestant and my husband was raised Jewish. We're looking for a place we can both feel comfortable."

"We grew up Catholic, but haven't gone to church in many years. Now we want our children to have some kind of religious education, but we don't want the kind of dogma we grew up with."

"My son wanted to go to church, so we're trying this one."

"I am gay/lesbian/bisexual/transgendered and have assumed until now there was no church that would welcome me. I heard you are open."

"My life is feeling empty, and I want to be reminded of 'what it's all about,' but I don't want God shoved down my throat."

"I believe in God, but I'm not comfortable in my childhood church."

"We are definitely not Christian. This place isn't Christian, is it?"

"I was recently divorced and am looking for a community."

"Some of the people I like and respect the most in town go to this church so I'm here to check it out."

"My father died and I realized I had nowhere to go for comfort."

"I have been a UU for many years and just moved to this area. I'm here to transfer into this congregation."

Reflecting on this list, it is clear that only the last one guarantees any knowledge of the history and heritage of Unitarian Universalism. My colleagues and I must explain many times that Unitarian Universalism is not a New Age religion. While we respect the personal spiritual search and exercise a radical theological flexibility, we also are a merger of two traditions, each of which existed for hundreds of years. The simplest way to explain it is that both Unitarians and Universalists grew out of the left wing of the Protestant Reformation. As such, we have clearly Christian roots.

We also have deeply American roots. In New England, many churches that are now Unitarian began as the first and only church in town, hence the number of "First Parishes" we have. Between 1820 and 1830, once the Unitarians had formally organized themselves, most of those First Parishes took either the Unitarian or the Congregationalist position, with the victor keeping the property and the loser building a new church, often right across the street. Our order of service has descended directly from our Puritan ancestors, and while it has evolved a fair bit over the generations, it still reflects the style of religion in colonial America.

A critical point in our history came with the life and work of Ralph Waldo Emerson. Emerson left the Unitarian ministry because it didn't allow him to think and speak as freely as he wished. In response, some wished to cross him off our rolls and maintain a narrow interpretation of Unitarian orthodoxy; however, his appeal was so great, to younger people especially, that this view didn't hold. Ultimately, we drew our circle wider, invited the Transcendentalists inside, and established ourselves as a people willing to consider new ideas, even if they transcended the bounds of Christianity.

That was in the mid-nineteenth century. In the intervening 150 years, we have made theological room for humanism, agnosticism, eastern influences, and feminist perspectives. In the process, we have become a more comfortable place for Jews as well. As a result, most of our congregations are now made up of people who respond to an eclectic mixture of religious metaphors. The underlying principle is respect for the integrity of each person's spiritual evolution: There is room here for you to express your highest truths in your own terms, and for that expression to change as your life experiences, reading, and thinking evolve.

A demon we fight, however, is that of being defined more by what we *are not* than what we *are*. Some people find us after having been wounded in some way by their earlier religious experiences, so the most important feature for them is that we are "not like X or Y." When on occasion we do draw from the metaphors of that tradition in a worship service, these people struggle.

"The only way this enterprise works," I often say, "is if we approach it with an attitude of religious maturity. You will hear reference to a wide range of theological viewpoints here, some of which will speak to you more than others. You will probably even hear some things that remind you of the place you left. The key to not just surviving but thriving in a UU context is to take in all of it, engage with that which touches you most directly, and either ignore or learn from the rest." Insisting on any orthodoxy will not fly in Unitarian Universalism, since we are grounded in theological liberty; and if we removed every reference that rubbed somebody the wrong way, we would be left with the worst kind of lowest-common-denominator mediocrity.

Religious maturity, as I am coming to understand it, means an acceptance of the idea that all religious language is the language of poetry and metaphor. If you have been wounded by religion in the past, it is your mission, should you choose to accept it, to come to peace with that irreversible part of your history. No church can take away the pain you have already suffered, but we can assure you that there are better experiences to be had. If you can separate your wound from the religious metaphor that was present when the wound occurred, then maybe words like "Christ," "sin," and "God" can become less toxic. In our church, these words are invitations into your soul, not threats held over your head.

Unitarian Universalist congregations do, on the whole, accept the idea that they need to change with the times. It is not a new idea that we must remain flexible in order to remain relevant, though to be sure, we manifest this understanding imperfectly. All the Alban

Institute's theories of congregational life and resistance to change apply to us as much as anyone. But the greater risk for Unitarian Universalists, I believe, is being too flexible, not too rigid. It is tempting for us to accommodate all requests and opinions in the name of respect for every person and our democratic faith. But if we try to be all things to all people, we will ultimately have no clear understanding of who we are.

In response to this risk, I have taken on much more of a role of "keeper of the tradition" than I anticipated. I read every bit of history of my almost-300-year-old congregation that I can find. I milk the veterans for stories. I weave bits of history—Unitarian, Universalist, and First Parish—into sermons. I teach classes on UU history and theology. I say no, sometimes, when people want to change our liturgy or style. I remind them why we do what we do, how we are structured, that there is a depth of tradition on which we stand. It is amazing to me, really, that I sometimes feel like a conservative voice in my very liberal church. I guess I am living out that old irony that when the critics become the establishment, they change their tune. But I am so sure that our risk is not so much death by rigidity as death by fragmentation, that I believe I am doing the right thing.

We Must Encourage the Lively Coexistence of Particular Spiritualities

At the same time, I do encourage a different kind of theological democracy in our church. If I am the keeper of the tradition on Sunday mornings, then I work in partnership with many subgroups of our church that delve into particular spiritualities at other times of the week. Groups meet for Zen meditation, women's spirituality,

Torah study, and Jesus scholarship. There are support groups for parents, men, women, people with aging parents, and young adults. There are various discussion and study and social groups, and several ways to make music. There is ample room for new gatherings to form and to meet voluntarily for as long as the commitment lasts. These groups strengthen our community by providing opportunities for people to deepen their spiritual lives in specific ways, while our Sunday service offers a more encompassing worship experience. The lively coexistence of all of these is an expression of our religious maturity.

The Ideal Church of the Future

Some interesting work has been done in the past ten years by liberal religionists who were willing to put theological differences aside and take a lesson from the fundamentalists. It did not escape our notice that it was the newer, nondenominational Christian groups that were growing explosively, producing "mega churches" that drew thousands through the doors every week. Although it is tempting for us to dismiss this phenomenon as playing to a dumbed-down public's desire for easy answers, I concur with those who believe there is more to it than that.

A study of those very large religious institutions suggests that they have several characteristics we can learn from: They are open and active twenty-four hours a day, seven days a week; they offer activities for small groups of every possible description; they offer a feeling of community that doesn't exist anywhere else in most people's lives; they offer inspiration to those who are struggling, as well as a sense of purpose to those who feel adrift, and they do it with spirit, enthusiasm, and fun.

These characteristics may be applied to any theological stance, and are particularly well-suited to our UU structure of congregational polity. Our congregations, with the right kind of motivation and leadership, can do all of these things. So here is a view of the church I envision:

It is a building with many beautiful and comfortable rooms. In each room there is a different group meeting—for mutual support, for social action, for spiritual development, for adult education, or for music. The spiritual development groups have Christian, Jewish, Buddhist, and feminist focuses; some are studying poetry, literature, art, and music from a spiritual point of view. In another room is a weekly prayer group. There are continuous gatherings to study the history of Unitarian Universalism and of this congregation. There are mid-week services for meditation and healing in a small chapel apart from the main sanctuary. There is an opportunity for people of every theological flavor to deepen spiritually.

There are choirs and musical groups for a variety of ages and excellent music at all worship services. The pews in the sanctuary are comfortable and the room is simple and beautiful. Sunday services are the center of church life, from which all else flows. These services are inspiring, thought-provoking, and comforting. There is a mix of music, silence, reading, and good preaching in the liturgy. People gather before and after services for an informal brunch.

There is a Friday night coffee house and frequent social programs, lectures, and films. The church is known for its support of local arts and social programs.

There is a kitchen attached to a hall where people often share a meal after work. There is age-appropriate child care available, and children participate in service projects and church activities early on. A vibrant Sunday School teaches children to be open-minded, thoughtful, clear in their own identity, oriented toward service and social justice, and comfortable with a diversity of people.

The liberal church I envision equally welcomes people of all ages and circumstances, whether single or partnered, parent or childless, gay or straight, black or white, new to the United States or blue-blooded Brahmin. The subgroups within this church function so well that someone knows when you have been sick or absent for awhile, and calls to see how you are.

This church did not set out to become large, but it grows because it functions so well. People like to be there. They feel understood and cared for and inspired there, and they have the satisfaction of being part of something greater than themselves that is a force for good in the world.

This is the Unitarian Universalist church I envision for the next century. Oh, and one more thing: This church has plenty of staff, both ordained and lay, with clearly outlined responsibilities and clear lines of authority, and full benefits. A person can dream, can't she . . . ?

As Ralph Waldo Emerson once said:

"A person will worship something—have no doubt about that. We may think our tribute is paid in secret in the dark recesses of our hearts—but it will out. That which dominates our imaginations and our thoughts will determine our lives, and character. Therefore, it behooves us to be careful what we worship, for what we are worshiping we are becoming."

May we have the spirit and the focus to become what we envision.

THE CHURCH AS MIDWIFE: USHERING IN LIFE AND HOPE

Sister Theresa Rickard

I was brought up in a large, middle class family in the suburbs of New York City. I am the fifth of six children. My parents were committed Catholic Christians. I attended Catholic schools and felt nurtured and strengthened

by my faith. I spent most of my grammar school years with my finger over my lips. I think it was the beginnings of my preaching ministry. However, at that time my teachers did not quite appreciate it! During my senior year in high school, my classmates awarded me the dual honor of being "most popular" and "most rowdy." I was no angel and spent more time developing my social and athletic skills than my academic prowess.

I attended a public college and was involved in campus ministry, volunteer work, and athletics. I dated throughout high school and college and was engaged to be married in my early twenties. I always had a deep feeling for God, valued my membership in the Catholic church, and had a great desire to serve the poor, but was uncertain about what to do with all this. I thought about being a nun off and on since grammar school, but did not think I would quite fit.

In my senior year of college, I had a deep experience of Jesus' personal love and call, and began to refocus and rearrange my priorities by putting God first in my life. For three years after graduating, I taught in a public high school. I then ministered for three years as a member of the Parish Mission Team of the Archdiocese of New York. I lived in a praying community with nuns, priests, and other young lay people, and traveled each week to a different parish where we offered spiritual renewal-preaching through personal stories, music, and meditations.

I realized that volunteering for a few years in church service was not enough. God was asking me to radically give over my life. At the age of twenty-six, I finally took the plunge and entered the Dominican Sisters of Blauvelt, New York. I began my life and ministry as a sister in the South Bronx, where I was shaped and formed by the people with whom I lived and ministered. My theological studies and graduate degrees from Fordham University and Union Theological Seminary in New York City, where I received a Master in Divinity, were opportunities to reflect theologically on my experience and hone my pastoral skills.

The people in the Bronx, whom I served and love, continue to shape my spirit and deepen my compassion. They warmly welcomed me into their hearts and families. They put up with my imperfect Spanish, lack of experience, and pale skin. They taught me about the variety of their cultures and invited me to bless their children and listen to their stories of brokenness and to their dreams for a better future. The Latinos served me rice and beans; the West Africans shared cola nuts with me and explained their tribal customs. I became minister, healer, godmother, confidant, friend, and most importantly, sister.

I am now a vocation minister for my Dominican Congregation, where I help young adults grow in their faith and discover ways to serve God. I am also a companion to those who are exploring a call to serve the church by becoming a Dominican Sister.

I also have a preaching ministry and offer retreats to a variety of people and age groups. In my preparation, I reflect on the community I will be addressing and I try to tap into their issues, values, and struggles. I share my faith, hoping to connect with their life. My prayer is that a word will inspire and lead them into the process of healing, forgiveness, and to a *deeper and more personal relationship with God through Jesus Christ.*

I spend my life contemplating the many manifestations of God in my daily

life and sharing the fruits of my contemplation with others.

> "Tell me. What is it you plan to do with your one wild
> and precious life?"
>
> *—Mary Oliver*

This question haunted me throughout my adolescence
and into my young adult years. It continues to challenge me as I
walk with God as a Roman Catholic nun. I have chosen to be a
minister in the Catholic Church as a Dominican Sister at a time
when many of my peers have rejected the institutional church and
do not consider a vocation as a Sister, Brother, or Priest to be a
viable option. Many think I'm crazy. For me, it has been the hardest
yet best decision I have made. It has given my "one wild and precious life" focus and expanded me in ways I never thought possible.
God continues to surprise me as each new day unfolds. My bound-
less energy has touched into the energy of God's Spirit. God continues to lead me to people and places I would have never known or
gone to.

I partied in college and played varsity sports. I was engaged to
be married. I run, bike, and love life. I have deep and long-standing
friendships with women and men, and I am close with my family. I
am crazy about my nieces and nephews. I struggle with celibacy. My
heart yearns when I hold a baby. One of our Sisters, who taught
high school in the Bronx, told her students one day, "No, you won't

die if you don't have sex. I stand before you as living, breathing proof." However, there are fleeting moments when I wonder.

I believe that being a nun is not about what I have given up. It is not about sacrifice. If that was the whole story, I would be long gone. A friend of mine once told me, "You don't want to be a nun because all that life is about is none of this and none of that." I did not become a Sister to do penance or to escape life. Instead, I became one to engage in life in a fuller way. I have a fire for God and a passionate desire to make a difference in our church and world. I am energized by being part of something greater than myself.

What It Means to Be a Nun

The vows of poverty, chastity, and obedience that I have embraced and continue to struggle with are vehicles of life for me. Sister Joan Chittister, a noted author, states, "What the world needs now, respects now, demands now, is not poverty, chastity, and obedience; it is generous justice, reckless love, and limitless listening." She does not mean we should abandon our traditional vows, but reinterpret them in a way that makes sense in today's world. The vows I took commit me to rail against the status quo and what most people in our world value. So I now understand poverty as sharing my life generously with others; I live a simple lifestyle, am committed to ecological stewardship, and have a deep concern for the poor. I believe in chastity as a radical love of God and all God's people, especially the marginalized and oppressed people of our world; and that obedience means attentively listening to God, my church, my religious order, and the needs of God's people. My vows give me a framework to shed the materialism, consumerism, and excessive individualism that permeate our society. While learning to do with a lot less, I have experienced not deprivation, but freedom and inner peace. I find joy in the simple things of life and continue to discover that more is not necessarily better. The spirituality behind these vows can be helpful to anyone seeking the spiritual life: living simply, loving faithfully, and listening to others, especially the poor.

People are surprised when they discover I am a Sister. They say, "You seem so normal." The media and caricatures of Sisters with a ruler in hand and a sour puss on their faces, or as naive and helpless somehow pervade the consciousness of people. A new plastic novelty named "nunzilla" that spits fire certainly does nothing to enhance our image as caring, justice-seeking women. Yes, some Sisters did act a bit like "nunzilla." Many were products of our society and church at that time. Some were overwhelmed by the classes of over sixty-five children that were placed before them. Talk about stress! But certainly there were more who have left a tremendous positive impact on many lives.

Sisters are intelligent, socially conscious, hard working, faith-filled women. We are as ordinary as most people, but are quite extraordinary in our commitment to the common good. We have shed the drama of our medieval garb, opened ourselves to the world, and fully immersed ourselves in life. We remain preachers, educators, social workers, and healers. However, we do it differently from the way it was done in the past.

Who we are as ministers and how we minister has changed radically. Our vocation as Sister does not make us holier than others, or put us on a higher plane. We have answered the call that comes from our baptism, a call to try to live holy lives and serve God's people in a unique way. We no longer see ourselves as the guardians of doctrine and dispensers of knowledge. We have come to recognize that virtue lies not in blind obedience but in the rigorous work of truth-seeking. Our hope is that we may be preachers of truth, facilitators of learning, healers of bodies and spirits, and collaborators in the work of the church.

Sister Donna Markham, a psychologist and author, writes that Sisters commit themselves to a vowed life in community in order to make a difference—for the poor, the oppressed, the vulnerable, and the abandoned in our world. Our commitment to living communally is in itself a witness in a world trying to become community. We believe in the mission of Jesus to promote justice and right relationships among peoples, between individuals and their God, and among all who dwell upon this planet.

What It Means to Be the Church: God's Compassionate Presence in the World

I have discovered that by using the metaphor of midwife, I can articulate best my vision of church and who we are called to be. I understand the church to be God's compassionate presence in the world, bringing forth life in the midst of struggle and pain. The church is not fundamentally about structures and buildings; it is a movement of people working together to facilitate life and hope in the world. The midwife is one who companions, listening attentively to the heartbeat of both the mother and child. She is self-possessed; she knows who she is and remains poised to react. The midwife is present to the mother in her pain and assists her in her struggle to usher in new life. The church and the people of God are called to be midwife for each other and for the world. This is my vision for the church and the sisterhood in the next century.

The profession of the midwife and the use of it as a metaphor to describe other realities is not new. We find stories of midwives in the Hebrew scriptures, and the Bible uses the metaphor of midwife to tell us something about God. In Psalm 22:9–10, we encounter God as midwife: "Yet it was you who took me from the womb; you kept me safe on my mother's breast." The "you" found in both lines is God, the compassionate one. Phyllis Trible, a noted biblical scholar, writes that it is God who draws the child from the womb and places the new life on the nurturing breast of the mother. Both the child and the mother are consoled. Essentially my vision of church is the people of God being compassionate witnesses in the world bringing forth life and hope. It is only possible to be bearers of hope and healing if we are grounded in God and if we nurture our inner life. Our union with God instills in us the energy and passion we need to be healers of our broken world and voices of justice for the oppressed.

I am a woman of the church, even though I struggle with the humanity of the church and its imperfections. I believe in an inclusive church that is essentially concerned about justice, charity, and the spiritual and temporal needs of people. I do not close my eyes when the church fails an individual or its people. Instead, I keep the issues raised with both hands and move forward on my feet. It is too easy to bail out of institutions or organizations when they fail us. The most effective way to initiate change is to stay in the struggle—motivated by love and not by bitterness. The goodness of the church, particularly at the grassroots, and the power to effect change in our society far outweighs the church's limitations and sometimes unjust behavior. Historically, we know the church is far from perfect, but our hope lies in the truth that the church is always in the process of renewing itself.

Creating Authentic Spirituality

Authentic spirituality is not just about inner peace and personal healing. I believe it entails a commitment to God and to a community of faith. Authentic spirituality calls us beyond ourselves to live our values, to love well, and to put on the mind and heart of God. A spirituality that is helpful to me comes from the founder of my religious order, a twelfth-century preacher named Dominic de Guzman. He instilled in his followers the spirituality of living a life of contemplation and sharing the fruits of one's contemplation with others. St. Dominic was deeply rooted in prayer, found life and strength in the word of God, was intensely involved in the issues of his times, and had a particular sensitivity to the poor. He went forth from his community and took to the streets, reaching out to the poor and preaching truth to those without hope. Dominic returned to his community for prayer, study, and support to be refueled—to enkindle his fire and regain his focus.

In the 1960s and 1970s, social activism became the faith response of many religious people. A commitment to solitude, prayer, and ritual were put aside. For many, their spirituality was based in action, and their works of justice and charity became their prayer. Some of these same folks in the late 1980s began to burn out, their inner resources were depleted, and they were left diminished and unfulfilled. For some people, belonging to a community of faith and worshiping regularly became secondary and the rituals that nourished them were rendered antiquated and out-dated.

Other religious people live their faith more privately and are focused on the correctness of ritual, loyalty to the institution, and attaining personal salvation. There are others who do not belong to an organized religion but are seeking a spiritual path that is grounded in self-fulfillment, inner peace, and positive thinking—often for their sake alone. These spiritualities usually come up short.

Everyone has a spirituality whether they call it that or not. We live in a frenzied world where getting ahead and having more possessions or wealth than our neighbor often becomes the basis of our spirituality. Life continues to pass us by, and we hardly notice. Time for personal reflection and quality time with friends and family becomes scarce. Some of these people attend church, but, yet, find it difficult to immerse themselves in the mystery of God. Instead, they spend their Sunday worship thinking about their next task or project. When our spirits are not nourished, they dry up, and our capacity for love, wonder, and awe is diminished.

As we move into the next millennium, we find younger people searching for God, for a sense of community, and ways to simplify their lives. They are also reaching out to those who are less fortunate. Dominic's spirituality, rooted in contemplation and sharing the fruit of one's contemplation with others, is one road to a deeper communion with God, self, and others. The contemplation that Dominic emphasized included both personal and communal contemplation. It was out of a prayerful spirit that Dominic sent his followers two by two to reach those in need and to share a word of hope with the despairing. Dominic reminded his followers to go with only one cloak on their backs and the Gospel of Matthew in their hands. That certainly makes travel less of a hassle and enables us to be more focused. A contemplative person has to develop habits of prayer, silence, and reflection. True contemplation in the spirit of Jesus leads women and men to "act justly, love tenderly and walk humbly with their God" (Micah 6:8).

Being a Contemplative in Action

The Catholic Church's role today must be to help us live a more contemplative life, to help us develop the skills we need to grow in our faith, and to challenge us to be a witness to the world of the gratuitous love of God for every person. When we move from a contemplative spirit into loving action, we can become midwives for others: facilitators of life and hope.

In the second book of the Bible, at the beginning of the Exodus story, we encounter two midwives, Shiphrah and Puah. They are not exactly household names, but they can shed some light on the church's call to be midwife. While the Israelites were slaves of the Egyptians, they were growing in strength and numbers. The Egyptian leaders were afraid that the Hebrews were growing too strong and would eventually revolt and possibly overthrow the Egyptians. The leaders formed a plan to kill all Jewish boys at birth. The Pharaoh instructed the Hebrew midwives to accomplish his diabolical deed. Two of these women reflected on their situation and refused to obey the royal command. They cunningly found a way to save the baby boys.

Shiphrah and Puah took their "one wild and precious life" and saved a people. These compassionate and courageous midwives did not cave in to the Pharaoh's death-dealing command. They moved beyond their self-interest and their fear that this heartless king would take his vengeance out on them. By sparing the male babies and thus saving Moses, they became facilitators of life and hope for the oppressed Hebrew people. In reality, the Exodus—the journey of the Hebrews from slavery to freedom—owes its beginning, not to Moses, but to these extraordinary women.

The midwives disobeyed Pharaoh because they were God-fearing women. Fear of God in the Bible means an experience of the holy. It also means to trust and revere God. In biblical religion, true love for God creates a sense of deep pain at the thought of doing evil. The fear of God implies a complete dependence on God, inspired by a profound commitment to God's will. The prophet Isaiah exhorts us not to fear human beings but to trust in the God who loved us into being:

> Do not fear, for I have saved you.
> I have called you by name and you are mine.
> When you pass through the water I will be with you;
> and through the rivers, they shall not overwhelm you;
> when you walk through fire you shall not be burned,
> and the flames shall not consume you.
> *(Isaiah 43:1–2)*

The midwives, imbued with the fear of God, walked through the waters of injustice and the fire of cruelty and were not overwhelmed. They stood before the birthstool of a new Israel and courageously acted to facilitate life and hope for God's people.

Creating Midwives to Change the World

It is the job of those of us in the church today to help show people how to be midwives—and change the world. Many ordinary people today are midwives of life and hope. They go about their daily lives loving, sacrificing for others, motivated by their love of God and their commitment to live a Christian life. I have been inspired by many midwives in my life, and I desire to be part of their company. I will share a story of one of the extraordinary midwives I met while living and ministering in the Bronx.

One of my early mentors was Antonia Diaz, an eighty-five year old Puerto Rican woman with a tough mind, incredible

perseverance, and a tender heart. Mrs. Diaz was an active parish-
ioner of Sacred Heart Catholic Church in the Highbridge section of
the Bronx. She became a community activist at the age of sixty.
Antonia knew what to do with her "one wild and precious life." In
1971, the neighborhood began to burn. Many people moved out.
The owner of Antonia's building, who had not paid taxes for years,
eventually abandoned the building. The tenants were receiving no
services, so they began to move out and squatters moved in. A number of these new settlers were drug dealers and users. Fear seized the
remaining families. Antonia, the oldest tenant, refused to leave. She
organized the remaining tenants and told them they could save the
building, but everyone had to pay rent. Antonia began collecting the
rent and hired a new superintendent. Those who refused to pay were
asked to leave. The building began to take on life. But soon, one of
the suspected drug dealers stopped paying rent. Antonia confronted
him, and he laughed when she demanded rent and told him he must
clean up his act. He told her, "Go home, old woman."

So she took him to court, and he was given seventy-two hours
to leave. He just ignored the order. Marshals arrived with two trucks
and removed all his expensive furniture and appliances. When he
came home that evening, he found his apartment sealed with a
shiny padlock. Filled with rage, he went straight for Mrs. Diaz,
threatening to kill her and torch the building. People were terrified
and the police advised her to leave town. Antonia went to her
daughter's home in Brooklyn; her daughter begged her to stay, but
within a few days, Antonia returned home. She prodded the police
and rallied the people.

Antonia resisted the drug lord's oppression; she refused to run
away. Once the drug lord lost his power over the people, smaller
dealers were forced out. Three years later, the city gave the building

to the people. The apartment house became the first cooperative in the neighborhood. Antonia, the facilitator of the process, is a midwife. She has helped to bring to birth something new—a vital community in the Bronx.

> From the beginning till now the entire creation, as we
> know, has been groaning in one great act of giving birth;
> and not only creation, but all of us who possess the first
> fruits of the spirit, we too groan inwardly as we wait for
> our bodies to be set free.
> *(Romans 8:22–23)*

Antonia, through the power of the spirit, heard the groaning of her community. She was attentive to the pulse of God in the heart of those remaining families. Their desire for life gave her hope as she labored with them to defy the drug lord and reclaim their building for a new community. Like those ancient midwives, she too feared God because she was in relationship with the all holy and awesome Creator. And because of that, she overcame her fear of the drug lord. Antonia could not do what she does if it were not for her faith commitment and the support of her Catholic community.

Antonia does not stand alone—she is part of something greater than herself. Antonia is a contemplative in action; she reflects on the needs of her community in light of her faith, and she acts. The fruits of her prayer are obvious.

Putting Our Energy into Birthing a New Community

The Catholic Church is a vehicle of grace that can energize us to be among the midwives charged with birthing a new community—which we call the reign of God. This is our charge.

The heart of Jesus' mission was to proclaim the coming of the reign of God by his words and by the way he lived his life. The energy and power of his vision emerged from his communion with God. Jesus moved from reaching out to the suffering crowd and into the silence of the hillside, the sea, and the garden. He was strengthened by the community that gathered around him and by the Jewish rituals that they celebrated together.

Christians, who profess to be followers of Christ, share in his life and mission. We create the reign of God wherever we find ourselves. The reign of God is the transforming presence of God calling us to oneness with all people and with all of creation. The work of my order—and indeed, any order of nuns—is the realization of Jesus' vision in ways that are best enfleshed through people who are both contemplatives and activists. We emerge from a contemplative stance toward life denouncing injustice, hatred, and evil, and announcing the good news of God's love revealed in the life, death, and resurrection of Jesus the Christ. Co-creators of God's reign do not condemn the world, point fingers at other people's immorality, castigate and isolate certain segments of our society, and blame "those" people for the breakdown of our families. Instead, they put their energy into transforming the world. Ushering in God's rule is about speaking the truth in love and inviting all into the vision of the peaceable kingdom. We cannot spend our energy claiming who is saved and who is not. I am relieved to know that judgment is God's business and not in the hands of human beings. I would rather take my chances with God.

The reign of God is not an abstract construct or something that will only be experienced when we die or when Jesus returns in glory. It is happening right now before our eyes, and people, through God's grace, are making it happen. The reign that Jesus ushered in is a revolutionary vision of the world that calls us to radically change our world view and the way we treat one another. We believe that Jesus was not just a nice guy who healed and comforted a few people. He was midwife to a holy revolution that cost him his life. Jesus ushered in the reign of God and transformed all of history. Those who dare to come to know him as their God and allow his spirit to fill them are called to continue the transforming process. All will not be well until justice is the norm for all people and peace and harmony reign in the soul of all creation. We must make this known, in word and deed.

The Catholic Church is a sacramental church, revealing the living God in earthy, ordinary ways. The image of midwife is easily identified with this church, which proclaims in word and sacrament that the ordinary reveals the power and mystery of God. God's presence and action surround us. God is mediated through all of creation; if only we would take the time to notice, to reflect, to stand in awe. A poem by Elizabeth Barrett Browning describes this reality:

Earth's crammed with heaven,
And every common bush afire with God;
And only [they] who see take off [their] shoes;
The rest sit round it and pluck blackberries.

Our Hands Are God's Hands

We stand on holy ground, and God's grace abounds on our living planet. This belief that God is revealed in the ordinary must lead us to contemplate God on the train, in those with whom we work, in the faces of the suffering, and in the delight of children—for the earth is crammed with heaven.

As Catholics, we must be shaped by the belief that the infinite is revealed in the finite. Everything God creates is good, whether directly or in partnership with us. Our view of the world is essentially positive, and we believe that like us, the world is more good than evil. We find goodness, kindness, and grace in unexpected places. We recognize God's presence, name it, bless it, and celebrate it. This understanding of God's presence discovered in the everyday can assist any spiritual seeker, regardless of her or his tradition; this will enhance our daily walk with God. If we cannot connect our experience of God with our daily struggle, God's power to work in our lives is diminished.

The faith of Catholic Christians is grounded in the belief that God's grace is mediated primarily through the sacramental life of the church. For Catholics, water refreshes and becomes a sign of new life; God is made present in bread and wine; God's healing and divine, forgiving love is communicated through the soothing touch of blest oil. God forgives through a listening ear and a human heart; God binds and blesses the commitment between a loving couple through an ordained minister of the church and the witness of the gathered community. We bless pregnant women and our friends before they leave on a long journey, and our Hispanic sisters and brothers bless their children before leaving their homes. We bless new homes, cars, animals, and gardens and we call upon the communion of saints to intercede in prayer for us in times of trouble.

Meister Eckhart, a thirteenth-century Dominican preacher and mystic, challenged his congregation by asking, "What good is it if Mary gave birth to the child of God fourteen hundred years ago, and I do not also give birth to Jesus in my time and culture? We are all mothers of God," Eckhart insisted, "for God is always needing to be born." It is through our contemplation that we become full with

God; a fullness that continues to expand only when we share it with others. We who have embraced the call to birth Jesus in our time and culture sing with Mary:

> My soul proclaims your greatness, O my God,
> and my spirit has rejoiced in you, my Savior,
> For your regard has blessed me, poor, and a serving woman.
> From this day all generations will call me blessed,
> For you who are mighty, have made me great.
> Most Holy be your name.
>
> *(Luke 1:46–7)*

We Must Use Our Gifts to Defy the Modern "Pharaohs" and Bring Forth the Reign of God

God's transforming work is ordinarily done through human hands, like a nun's hands, or your hands. We are called to cooperate with God's grace and use our God-given talents for the common good. We can make a difference and affect our world in a positive way. We are the new midwives called to stand up to the modern pharaohs and to use our gifts to bring forth the reign of God.

Over 3,000 years have passed since the time of Shiphrah and Puah and over 2,000 years since the time of Jesus. Yet modern pharaohs continue to threaten our lives, the lives of our children, the lives of women, the sanctity of marriage, our families, our communities, the vibrancy and future of our churches and synagogues. Who are the pharaohs within us and surrounding us who rob us of our love for God and others, who strip us of inner peace and separate us from our souls? Who will stand up and continue the tradition of the midwives and the many saints who have blessed our world? Who will continue the works of women of faith like Antonia?

Nancy Hastings Sehested, a Protestant minister and noted

preacher, has also asked, "Who are our pharaohs?" She answers that our pharaohs are our pessimism and cynicism that paralyze or lull us into accepting the status quo or keep us from seeking God. They are our addictions to drugs, alcohol, overeating, and gambling that numb us to life. The sins of racism, sexism, and anti-Semitism all foster hatred and keep us from communion with God and one another. The pharaohs of prejudice and intolerance inflict violence and isolation on homosexuals, the emotionally or physically handicapped, and on anyone who is different or considered useless.

We encounter the oppressing spirit of pharaoh in those who publicly disregard the plight of immigrants and poor people for the sake of political advancement. We recognize his spirit in transnational corporations that exploit laborers, particularly women and children who slave in factories without union protection. Excessive consumerism crushes our spirits, numbs us to the simple pleasures of life, and cultivates incessant greed.

We sometimes find pharaoh in those who profess love for us; in people who abuse us verbally or physically and are always putting us down. In people who mock commitment and herald sex without relationship and responsibility. Often the most insidious thieves of our life and freedom are ourselves—fears control us and lies infect our souls. Inner voices tell us, "You are not worth anything," "You can't change," "You are unlovable," and "Life is without hope."

How do we defy these pharaohs and summon the courage to choose a life that makes a difference? We cannot do it alone. It is only through the power of God within that we discover our own power and potential. The community of faith, in particular spiritual mentors, are there to support us and to companion us. It is up to us to be serious about our spiritual quest and to make a commitment—to put a stake in the ground.

We must be midwives like Shiphrah and Puah, who defy pharaoh. We resist and confront the injustice of the powerful. We weather apathy, fatalism, and individualism. We balk at a life devoid of meaning, distant from God, and centered on self. We—women and men both—refuse to let others shape the future of our communities, our country, our churches. Midwives are convinced about what to do with their "one wild and precious life." In them we encounter contemplatives in action who know who they are and whose they are.

We are part of the company of the new midwives, who defy the evil power of their age and choose to be facilitators of life and hope for their communities. Mother Mary Ann Sammon, who founded the Dominican Sisters of Blauvelt, also started an orphanage for homeless children over 100 years ago without any resources but her faith and a heart moved by the plight of orphaned children. Dorothy Day, who founded the Catholic Worker movement, lived and ate with people who were poor and broken. Daniel Berrigan, a Jesuit priest, led movements that protested the Vietnam war and the escalation of nuclear arms. For this, he was jailed many times. Archbishop Oscar Romero of El Salvador left the comfort of the bishop's study to be a voice for the poor. He was gunned down because of the truth he spoke. Mother Teresa left the security of teaching upper-class students and moved to the streets to care for the poorest of the poor in Calcutta. Pope John Paul II, with a body worn and ailing, courageously speaks for economic justice for the poorest people of our world and for religious freedom. At the dawn of the new millennium, he is calling for a year of jubilee, exhorting our world leaders to cancel the debt of developing countries and to end the death penalty.

Many of these women and men have fought with church

officials, their religious leaders, and government officials. They have struggled with the disapproval of friends and family; they stepped out of their traditional roles, and stretched the boundaries of what is considered the religious sphere. They are all women and men with a mission, and within the context of the Catholic community, they have lived lives that mattered. They have a fire in their belly and are willing to put a stake in the ground.

The company of midwives moves beyond my own Catholic community. Rosa Parks defied pharaoh by refusing to move to the back of the bus. Yitzchak Rabin worked tirelessly for the peace process in the Middle East. Nelson Mandela led the fight against apartheid and facilitated the birth of a new nation with reconciliation as its birth mark. Princess Diana overcame her personal struggles and pain to reach out to others through her charitable works.

These symbolic midwives witness to us that through the power of God, it is possible to defy the pharaohs who try to dominate us. They proclaim through their lives that the weakest and most broken among us has the possibility of greatness. We are inspired by their example and strengthened in our faith in God, the one who brings to birth life and hope in us; the God who is midwife to each of us and all of creation. The Psalmist sings to us of God as midwife:

> Yet it was you who took me from the womb;
> you kept me safe upon my mother's breasts.
> Upon you was I cast from my birth,
> since my mother's womb you have been my God.
> Be not far from me in my distress;
> there is no one else to help me.
>
> *(Psalm 22:9–11)*

We Are a Church Full of Our Possibilities

The God who delivered us into our mother's arms desires to deliver us into God's maternal presence. God leads us into a household of faith, an inner security; and from death to life.

We have the power to say "no" to death and "yes" to God. God is on our side and wants us to live full and abundant lives. It is God's will for us. Jesus proclaims to us: "I came so that you may have life, and have it more abundantly" (John 10:10). It is the role of the Catholic Church to make this plain. As we walk with God and open ourselves to God's transforming presence, our spirits will be set free to fly with the birds.

I am reminded of a recent afternoon I spent with my seven-year-old niece, Marifaith. She is quite a character, always collecting rocks, insects, and other creepy little objects and sticking them in her pockets. This day, she dug into her oversized school uniform and pulled out a large shiny rock in the shape of an egg. I was relieved that this time it was not something that flew or squirmed. She asked me, "Aunt Terry, is this a lucky rock or a wishing rock?" Without much thought, I said, "I think it is a lucky rock." "Oh rats," she spontaneously responded, "I was hoping for a wishing rock." She continued, "Oh, how I wish I could fly." "Marifaith, when you become older, you could be a pilot and fly a plane." She gave me a bewildered look. "No, Aunt Terry. Don't you understand? I want to fly like a bird." Marifaith, still fresh from God, has an active imagination and a creative spirit. Our imagination is what enables wishing. When we no longer wish or desire our hope is lost. Marifaith reminds me that, with God, we dwell in possibility.

We must see with the eyes of God and look beyond people's behavior and see their potential and possibilities. We grow in the spiritual life when we are attentive to the many manifestations of God in our daily lives and reach out to others with a word of hope. We also must ask the hard questions: Why do some people have so little? How does my consumerism affect others? What action can we take? Living a committed Christian life is about being politically involved; it means influencing policies that affect people's lives, especially those who are voiceless. If the church does not defend the sacredness of life, who will? This often means taking unpopular stands against abortion, the death penalty, and euthanasia, and for people who are poor and excluded. These stands will open us to being misunderstood and condemned by both the left and the right. But if we never put a stake in the ground, we will never stir up anyone or anything.

What Will You Do With Your One Wild and Precious Life?

There is room in organized religion for spiritual seekers who are critical thinkers and socially conscious. Most of all, we need those who are courageous enough to be midwives of a new Catholic Church—a community of faith that is inclusive and justice-seeking. Not a church of "fuzzy" feelings or one that condones all our behaviors, but a church that accepts people where they are, listens to their stories, and invites them to a change of heart.

We defy the pharaohs in our lives, not because we are women or men, or because we are black, brown, yellow, or white, or Catholic, Protestant, Jewish, Muslim, or Buddhist. We defy oppressors because of our relationship with God, Who is our power, our life, and our hope.

We are the new midwives. We are Shiphrah and Puah. We are

Antonia Diaz. We are Dorothy Day. We are Archbishop Romero. We are Mother Teresa. We are Nelson Mandela. We stand at the birth-stool of our communities. Let us defy pharaoh and obey God. Let us join the company of the midwives. Let us be about the birthing of a new community—contemplating and sharing the fruits of our contemplation with a world hungering for God.

Tell me. What is it you plan to do with your one wild and precious life?

For More Information

Catholic Network of Volunteer
  Service
4121 Harewood Road, NE
Washington, DC 20017-1593
Tel: (202) 529-1100 or
  (800) 543-5046
Fax: (202) 526-1094
E-mail: CNVS@ari.net
Website: www.cnvs.org

The Dominican Order
Sr. Terry Rickard OP,
  Blauvelt Dominican Sisters
496 Western Highway
Blauvelt, NY 10913
Tel: (914) 359-0696
E-mail: rickardt@opblauvelt.org
  or tarop@aol.com
Website: www.op.org and
  www.opblauvelt.org

Pax Christi U.S.A., International
  Catholic Peace Movement
532 W. 8th Street
Erie, PA 16502-1343
Tel: (814) 453-4955
Website:
  www.nonviolence.org/pcusa

National Catholic Young Adult
  Ministry Association
7541 W. Broadway Avenue
Forest Lake, MN 55025
Tel: (888) 629-2621

Network, A National Catholic
  Social Justice Lobby
801 Pennsylvania Avenue, SE,
  Suite 460
Washington, DC 20003-2167
Tel: (202) 547-5556
E-mail:
  network@networklobby.org
Website: www.networklobby.org

National Teens Encounter Christ
   Conference (TEC)
618 East 18th Street
Des Moines, IA 50316-3695
Tel: (515) 266-3893
E-mail: nateconf@netins.net

Religious Orders (Brothers,
   Sisters, Priests) and Diocesan
   Priesthood
Website: www.visionguide.org
   (Religious Orders)
Website:
   www.catholicforum.com/ncdvd
   (Diocesan Priesthood)

Retreats International, Inc.
Box 1067
Notre Dame, IN 46556
Tel: (219) 631-5320

CONTRIBUTORS

Lynn and Mark Barger Elliott, 34 and 32, serve as associate pastors at the First Presbyterian Church in Ann Arbor, Michigan. Lynn received her B.A. from Wheaton College and Mark holds a B.A. from Cornell University. Both earned their M.Div. degrees from Princeton Theological Seminary. They have worked in a variety of congregational and pastoral settings, including chaplaincy programs at prisons and hospitals.

Brad R. Braxton, 30, is the senior pastor of Douglas Memorial Community Church in Baltimore, Maryland. He earned a B.A. in religious studies from the University of Virginia and an M.Phil. from the University of Oxford (where he was a Rhodes Scholar), and is currently completing a Ph.D. at Emory University. Braxton was ordained as a Baptist minister in 1991 at the First Baptist Church in Salem, Virginia.

Norman Fischer, 51, is the co-abbot of the San Francisco Zen Center. He graduated from the Iowa Writers' Workshop in 1970, earned his M.A. in Buddhist studies from the Graduate Theological Union in Berkeley, California, and was ordained as a Zen priest by the Zen Center in 1980. Fischer is also a poet and author, and has taught about Buddhism in lectures and workshops to professional and religious audiences across the country. He is the chair of the Zen Hospice Project, and has participated with the Dalai Lama in conferences on Buddhist-Christian dialogue and nonviolence.

Niles E. Goldstein, 33, is the founding rabbi of The New Shul in New York City, a program officer/educator at the Jewish Life Network, and an associate of CLAL: the National Jewish Center for Learning and Leadership. He earned a B.A. in philosophy from the University of Pennsylvania and a M.A.H.L. and rabbinic ordination from the Hebrew Union College–Jewish Institute of Religion in New York. Goldstein is the voice behind "Ask the Rabbi" for Microsoft and is the National Jewish Chaplain for the Federal Law Enforcement Officers Association. He has written for *Newsweek* and other publications, is the editor of *Contact* and the author or editor of three books—*Forests of the Night: The Fear of God in Early Hasidic Thought, Judaism and Spiritual Ethics,* and *Duties of the Soul: The Role of Commandments in Liberal Judaism.* He is completing a book about finding God at the edge.

Brett C. Hoover, 32, is associate pastor at Church of St. Paul the Apostle in New York City. He received a B.A. in English and psychology from University of California at Santa Barbara, and an M.A. in theology from Washington Theological Union. Hoover helped revive the campus ministry program at the University of California at Berkeley, where he served as campus minister. He is the author of *Losing Your Religion, Finding Your Faith: Spirituality for Young Adults* and the co-editor of *Morning Praise, Evening Prayer.*

Yosef Kanefsky, 36, currently serves as rabbi of Congregation B'nai David-Judea in Los Angeles, California. He received his M.A. in Jewish history from Yeshiva University in New York, where he was ordained in 1989. Kanefsky was earlier the associate rabbi at the Hebrew Institute of Riverdale, New York, one of the national flagships of modern Jewish Orthodoxy. He has focused much of his rabbinic work on Jewish pluralism, enhancing the role of women in contemporary Orthodox Judaism, and social action.

Gregory Wm. M. Kimura, 31, is vicar of Holy Spirit Episcopal Church in Eagle River, Alaska. He holds a B.A. in philosophy and theology from Marquette University and a M.Div. from the Harvard Divinity School. Kimura was ordained an Episcopal priest by the Diocese of Alaska in 1994, and is chaplain to Alaska Pacific University and the University of Alaska at Anchorage. He will be studying toward a Ph.D. in theology at the University of Cambridge. He is a fourth-generation Japanese-American.

Stephanie R. Nichols, 37, is the senior minister of First Parish in Framingham, Massachusetts. She earned her B.A. in mathematics and religion from Dartmouth College and a M.Div. from Starr King School for the Ministry. Nichols has served congregations in Worcester, Massachusetts; Fresno, California; and Philadelphia, Pennsylvania. She has also been the Unitarian Universalist chaplain at Wellesley College. She is active in the causes of peace and women's rights.

Sara Paasche-Orlow, 32, is a program officer/educator at the Jewish Life Network and the former director of the Bavli Yerushalmi Project at the Jewish Community Center of the Upper West Side. She earned a B.A. from Oberlin College and has studied at the Free University in Berlin, the Hebrew University in Jerusalem, and the Pardes Institute of Jewish Studies in Jerusalem. Paasche-Orlow was ordained by Tsphe Jewish Theological Seminary in New York.

Theresa Rickard, 42, is the director of formation of new members at the Sisters of St. Dominic Convent in Blauvelt, New York. She received a B.A. in physical education from Springfield College, an M.A. in religion from Fordham University, and a M.Div. from Union Theological Seminary. Rickard professed final vows as a Catholic nun at St. Dominic's. She has worked extensively with the Archdiocese of New York and several parishes in the South Bronx.

About SKYLIGHT PATHS Publishing

Through spirituality, our religious beliefs are increasingly becoming *a part of our lives*, rather than *apart from* our lives. Nevertheless, while many people are more interested than ever in spiritual growth, they are less firmly planted in *traditional* religion. To deepen their relationship to the sacred, people want to learn from their own and other faith traditions, in new ways.

SkyLight Paths sees both believers and seekers as a community that increasingly transcends traditional boundaries of religion and denomination. Many people want to learn from each other, *walking together, finding the way.*

The SkyLight Paths staff is made up of people of many faiths. We are a small, highly committed group of people, a reflection of the religious diversity that now exists in most neighborhoods, most families. We will succeed only if our books make a difference in your life.

We at SkyLight Paths take great care to produce beautiful books that present meaningful spiritual content in a form that reflects the art of making high quality books. Therefore, we want to acknowledge those who contributed to the production of this book.

PRODUCTION
Marian B. Wallace & Bridgett Taylor

EDITORIAL & PROOFREADING
Sandra Korinchak & Martha McKinney

JACKET ART & DESIGN
Tom Nihan, Gloucester, Massachusetts

TEXT DESIGN
Graphic Identity, Inc., Brookfield, Connecticut

PRINTING AND BINDING
Lake Book, Melrose Park, Illinois

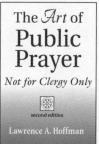

Other Interesting Books—Spirituality

WHO IS YOUR GOD?
An Innovative Guide to Finding Your Spiritual Identity
Created by *the Editors at SkyLight Paths*
Introduction by *Dr. John Berthrong, author of* The Divine Deli

An innovative guide to spiritual self-discovery.

This dynamic resource is designed to help you discover your own spiritual identity, providing a helpful framework to begin or deepen your spiritual growth. Begin by taking the unique spiritual identity self-test; tabulate your results; then explore one, two or more of the 34 faiths/spiritual paths represented.

6" x 9", 156 pp. Quality Paperback Original, ISBN 1-893361-08-X **$15.95**

SPIRITUAL MANIFESTOS
Visions for Renewed Religious Life in America from Young Spiritual Leaders of Many Faiths
Edited by *Niles Elliot Goldstein*
Preface by *Martin E. Marty*

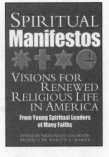

iscover how our faith traditions are being transformed by today's young spiritual leaders, who are beginning to remove the reasons why so many people have ept organized religion at arm's length. Here, ten contributors, most in their midirties, who span the spectrum of religious traditions—Protestant, Catholic, wish, Buddhist, Unitarian Universalist—present the innovative ways they are ansforming our spiritual communities and our lives.

These ten articulate young spiritual leaders engender hope for the vitality of 21st-century religion."
—Forrest Church, Minister of All Souls Church
in New York City

6" x 9", 256 pp. Hardcover, ISBN 1-893361-09-8 **$21.95**

THE NEW MILLENNIUM SPIRITUAL JOURNEY
Change Your Life—Develop Your Spiritual Priorities with Help from Today's Most Inspiring Spiritual Teachers
Created by *the Editors at SkyLight Paths*

A life-changing resource for reimagining your spiritual life.

What better time than now to refocus ourselves on what is most important in life? This book will allow you to set your own course of self-examination, reflection and spiritual transformation—with the help of self-tests, spirituality "exercises," sacred texts from many traditions, time capsule pages, and helpful suggestions from more than 20 spiritual teachers.

7" x 9", 144 pp. Quality Paperback Original, ISBN 1-893361-05-5 **$16.95**

Other Interesting Books—Spirituality

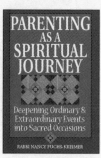

PARENTING AS A SPIRITUAL JOURNEY
Deepening Ordinary & Extraordinary Events into Sacred Occasions
by *Rabbi Nancy Fuchs-Kreimer*

A perfect gift for the new parent, and a helpful guidebook for those seeking to re envision family life. Draws on experiences of the author and over 100 parents c many faiths, revealing the transformative spiritual adventure that parents ca experience while bringing up their children. Rituals, prayers, and passages fro sacred Jewish texts—as well as from other religious traditions—are wove throughout the book.

"This is really relevant spirituality. I love her book."
—Sylvia Boorstein, author of *It's Easier Tha You Think* and mother of four

6″ x 9″, 224 pp. Quality Paperback, ISBN 1-58023-016-4 **$16.95**

THE EMPTY CHAIR: FINDING HOPE & JOY
Timeless Wisdom from a Hasidic Master, Rebbe Nachman of Breslov
Adapted by Moshe Mykoff and the Breslov Research Institute

A "little treasure" of aphorisms and advice for living joyously and spiritually today, written 200 years ago, but startlingly fresh in meaning and use. Challenges and helps us to move from stress and sadness to hope and joy. Teacher, guide, and spiritual master Rebbe Nachman provides vital words of inspiration and wisdom for life today for people of any faith, or of no faith.

"For anyone of any faith, this is a book of healing and wholeness, of being alive!"
—*Bookviews*

•AWARD WINNEI

4″ x 6″, 128 pp., 2-color text, Deluxe Paperback, ISBN 1-879045-67-2 **$9.95**

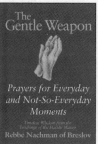

THE GENTLE WEAPON
Prayers for Everyday and Not-So-Everyday Moments
Timeless Wisdom from the Teachings of Rebbe Nachman of Breslov
by *Moshe Mykoff* and *S.C. Mizrahi*, together with the *Breslov Research Institute*

A small treasury of prayers that will open your heart and soul and give voice your deepest yearnings. A source of comfort for those in search of an upliftin perspective on life, using the warm insights and generous wisdom of Hasidic ma ter Rebbe Nachman of Breslov.

4″ x 6″, 144 pp., 2-color text, Deluxe Paperback, ISBN 1-58023-022-9 **$9.95**

GOD WHISPERS
Stories of the Soul, Lessons of the Heart
by *Karyn D. Kedar*

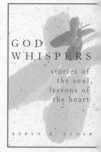

Eloquent stories from the lives of ordinary people teach readers that the joy and pain in our lives have meaning and purpose, and that by fully embracing life's highs and lows we can enrich our spiritual well-being. Helps us cope with difficulties such as divorce and reconciliation, illness, loss, conflict and forgiveness, loneliness and isolation.

6″ x 9″, 176 pp. Hardcover, ISBN 1-58023-023-7 **$19.95**

Other Interesting Books—Spirituality

FINDING JOY
A Practical Spiritual Guide to Happiness
by *Dannel I. Schwartz* with *Mark Hass*

Searching for happiness in our modern world of stress and struggle is common; *finding* it is more unusual. This guide explores and explains how to find joy through a time-honored, creative—and surprisingly practical—approach based on the teachings of Jewish mysticism and Kabbalah.

> "Lovely, simple introduction to Kabbalah. . . . A singular contribution."
> —American Library Association's *Booklist*

6" x 9", 192 pp. Quality Paperback, ISBN 1-58023-009-1 **$14.95**
Hardcover, ISBN 1-879045-53-2 **$19.95**

AWARD WINNER●

EYES REMADE FOR WONDER
A Lawrence Kushner Reader
Introduction by *Thomas Moore*, author of *Care of the Soul* and other books

A treasury of insight from one of the most creative spiritual thinkers in America. Whether you are new to Kushner or a devoted fan, his insights will stir your soul. With samplings from each of Kushner's works, and a generous amount of new material, this is a book to be savored, to be read and reread, each time discovering deeper layers of meaning in our lives. Offers something unique to both the spiritual seeker and the committed person of faith.

6" x 9", 240 pp. Quality Paperback, ISBN 1-58023-042-3 **$16.95**
Hardcover, ISBN 1-58023-014-8 **$23.95**

INVISIBLE LINES OF CONNECTION
Sacred Stories of the Ordinary
by *Lawrence Kushner*

Through his everyday encounters with family, friends, colleagues and strangers, Kushner takes us deeply into our lives, finding flashes of spiritual insight in the process. This is a book where literature meets spirituality, where the sacred meets the ordinary, and, above all, where people of all faiths, all backgrounds can meet one another and themselves. Kushner ties together the stories of our lives into a roadmap showing how everything "ordinary" is supercharged with meaning—*if* we can just see it.

6" x 9", 160 pp. Quality Paperback, ISBN 1-879045-98-2 **$15.95**
Hardcover, ISBN 1-58023-52-4 **$21.95**

NEW
ANNIVERSARY
EDITION

HONEY FROM THE ROCK
An Introduction to Jewish Mysticism
by *Lawrence Kushner*

Quite simply the easiest introduction to Jewish
mysticism you can read.

An introduction to the ten gates of Jewish mysticism and how they apply to daily life.

6" x 9", 176 pp. Quality Paperback, ISBN 1-58023-073-3 **$15.95**

Children's Spirituality

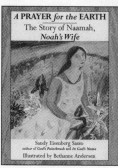

A PRAYER for the EARTH
The Story of Naamah,
Noah's Wife

Sandy Eisenberg Sasso
author of *God's Paintbrush* and *In God's Name*
Illustrated by Bethanne Andersen

•AWARD WINNER•

A PRAYER FOR THE EARTH
The Story of Naamah, Noah's Wife
by *Sandy Eisenberg Sasso*   **For ages 4 and**
Full-color illustrations by *Bethanne Andersen*

NONDENOMINATIONAL, NONSECTARIAN

This new story, based on an ancient text, opens readers' religious imagi·
tions to new ideas about the well-known story of the Flood. When God t·
Noah to bring the animals of the world onto the ark, God *also* calls
Naamah, Noah's wife, to save each plant on Earth.

9" x 12", 32 pp. Hardcover, Full-color illus., ISBN 1-879045-60-5 **$16.95**

THE 11TH COMMANDMENT
Wisdom from Our Children
For all ages   by *The Children of America*

MULTICULTURAL, NONDENOMINATIONAL, NONSECTARIAN

"If there were an Eleventh Commandment, what would it be?"

Children of many religious denominations across America answer this
question—in their own drawings and words.

8" x 10", 48 pp. Hardcover, Full-color illus., ISBN 1-879045-46-X **$16.95**

The **11th**
Commandment

Wisdom from Our Children
by The Children of America

•AWARD WINNER·

In Our Image
God's First Creatures

by Nancy Sohn Swartz
Illustrated by Melanie Hall

•AWARD WINNER•

IN OUR IMAGE
God's First Creatures
by *Nancy Sohn Swartz*   **For ages 4 and up**
Full-color illustrations by *Melanie Hall*

Selected as Outstanding by Parent Council, Ltd.™

NONDENOMINATIONAL, NONSECTARIAN

A playful new twist to the Creation story. Celebrates the interconnected-
ness of nature and the harmony of all living things.

9" x 12", 32 pp. Hardcover, Full-color illus., ISBN 1-879045-99-0 **$16.95**

FOR HEAVEN'S SAKE
For ages 4 and up
by *Sandy Eisenberg Sasso*
Full-color illustrations by *Kathryn Kunz Finney*

MULTICULTURAL, NONDENOMINATIONAL, NONSECTARIAN
"For heaven's sake, Isaiah!"

People said "for heaven's sake" to Isaiah a lot. Everyone talked about heaven.
"Thank heavens." "Heaven forbid." "For heaven's sake, Isaiah." But no one
would say what heaven was or how to find it.

So Isaiah decided to find out where heaven is. After seeking answers from many
different people, he found that heaven wasn't so difficult to find after all.

9" x 12", 32 pp. Hardcover, Full-color illus., ISBN 1-58023-054-7 **$16.95**

For Heaven'
Sak

Sandy Eisenberg Sasso
author of *God's Paintbrush* and *God Is in*
illustrated by
Kathryn Kunz Finney

Children's Spirituality

BUT GOD REMEMBERED
Stories of Women from Creation to the Promised Land

For ages 8 and up

by *Sandy Eisenberg Sasso*
Full-color illustrations by *Bethanne Andersen*

NONDENOMINATIONAL, NONSECTARIAN

A fascinating collection of four different stories of women only briefly mentioned in biblical tradition and religious texts, but never before explored. Award-winning author Sasso brings to life the intriguing stories of Lilith, Serach, Bityah, and the Daughters of Z, courageous and strong women from ancient tradition. All teach important values through their faith and actions.

AWARD WINNER•   9" x 12", 32 pp. Hardcover, Full-color illus., ISBN 1-879045-43-5 **$16.95**

IN GOD'S NAME

ages 4 and up

by *Sandy Eisenberg Sasso*
Full-color illustrations by *Phoebe Stone*

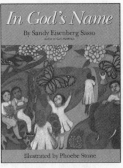

Selected as Outstanding by Parent Council, Ltd.™

MULTICULTURAL, NONDENOMINATIONAL, NONSECTARIAN

In God's Name tells the story of people who set out to find God's name. Celebrates the ultimate harmony of belief in one God by people of all faiths.

9" x 12", 32 pp. Hardcover, Full-color illus.,
ISBN 1-879045-26-5 **$16.95**

WHAT IS GOD'S NAME?

•AWARD WINNER•

An abridged board book version, for children ages 0–4.

5" x 5", 20 pp. Board, Full-color illus., ISBN 1-893361-10-1 **$7.95**

---

ages 4 and up

GOD IN BETWEEN

by *Sandy Eisenberg Sasso*
Full-color illustrations by *Sally Sweetland*

MULTICULTURAL, NONDENOMINATIONAL, NONSECTARIAN

If you wanted to find God, where would you look?
magical, mythical tale that teaches that God can be found where we are: thin all of us and the relationships between us.

9" x 12", 32 pp. Hardcover, Full-color illus., ISBN 1-879045-86-9 **$16.95**

•AWARD WINNER•

For ages 4 and up

GOD'S PAINTBRUSH

by *Sandy Eisenberg Sasso*
Full-color illustrations by *Annette Compton*

MULTICULTURAL, NONDENOMINATIONAL, NONSECTARIAN

Invites children of all faiths and backgrounds to encounter God openly in their own lives. Wonderfully interactive, provides questions adult and child can explore together at the end of each episode.

•AWARD WINNER•   11" x 8½", 32 pp. Hardcover, Full-color illus., ISBN 1-879045-22-2 **$16.95**

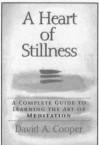